FOOTPRINTS OF AN ANGEL

FOOTPRINTS OF AN ANGEL

EPISODES FROM A JOINT AUTOBIOGRAPHY

SIEGFRIED E. FINSER

Lindisfarne Books | 2012

LINDISFARNE BOOKS | 2012
An imprint of SteinerBooks / Anthroposophic Press, Inc.
610 Main Street, Great Barrington, MA 01230
www.steinerbooks.org

Copyright © 2012 by Siegfried E. Finser

All rights reserved. No part of this book may be reproduced in any form without the written permission of the publishers, except for brief quotations embodied in critical articles and reviews.

COVER & BOOK DESIGN: WILLIAM JENS JENSEN

LIBRARY OF CONGRESS CATALOGING-IN-PUBLICATION DATA

Finser, Siegfried E.
  Footprints of an Angel : episodes from a joint autobiography / Siegfried E. Finser.
    p. cm.
  ISBN 978-1-58420-123-6 (paperback) —
  ISBN 978-1-58420-132-8 (hardcover) —
  ISBN 978-1-58420-124-3 (ebook)
  1. Self. 2. Awareness. 3. Angels. I. Title.
  BF697.F474 2012
  299'.935092—dc23
  [B]
                                                    2012007909

Contents

Introduction ... vii

SECTION ONE: SPACE AND TIME

1. Episode 1: First Encounter ... 3
2. Commentary on Space ... 6
3. First Conclusions about Angel Behavior ... 10
4. Episode 2: What's Good, What's Bad? ... 15
5. Second Conclusions about Angel Behavior ... 20
6. Episode 3: I Find Myself (maybe) ... 24
7. Third Conclusions about Angel Behavior ... 27

SECTION TWO: MY ANGEL TURNS ME LOOSE

8. Episode 4: On My Own ... 33
9. Episode 5: Selling Religion ... 37
10. Episode 6: The Facts of Life ... 40
11. Episode 7: Human Nature ... 45
12. Episode 8: Just a Joke ... 51
13. Episode 9: Shocking Success ... 54
14. Commentary on Turning Points in Life ... 58
15. Fourth Conclusions about Angel Behavior ... 63

SECTION THREE: ANGEL ASSISTED EDUCATION

16. Episode 10: A College Education with Pay ... 67
17. Episode 11: Sex Education ... 80
18. Episode 12: Romance ... 84
19. Episode 13: Love ... 88

20.	Episode 14: The Annunciation	91
21.	Episode 15: The Rainbow	98
22.	Commentary about How Angels Collaborate	102
23.	Fifth Conclusions about Angel Behavior	109

SECTION FOUR: ANGEL CHOREOGRAPHY

24.	Episode 16: Finding a Profession	115
25.	Commentary about Angel Footprints	135

SECTION FIVE: AMONG THE MIGHTY AND POWERFUL

26.	Episode 17: All about Power	139
27.	Episode 18: All about Powerlessness	147
28.	Episode 19: First Accident in Europe	152
29.	Episode 20: Second Accident in Europe	156
30.	Episode 21: Third Accident in Europe	161
31.	Commentary about Angel Power and Dreams	164
32.	Episode 22: The Golden Star Philosophy	166

SECTION SIX: HOME AT LAST

33.	Episode 23: Coming Home	173
34.	Episode 24: The Big Three Visit	181
35.	Episode 25: Birth of RSF Social Finance	188
36.	Commentary about Angel Choreography	199
37.	Sixth Conclusions: Believing Is Seeing	206

SECTION SEVEN: BACK IN SCHOOL!

38.	Episode 26: The Last Lesson	211

Introduction

In November 2007 I completed the book *Money Can Heal*. In several of the chapters I made reference to my Angel. I found myself forced to mention her in connection with certain biographical events.

It all began when I was able to overcome my arrogance and looked more closely at several meaningful events in my life. I don't know how I could have been so foolish as to think I had accomplished them alone. In looking back over the details it seemed so obvious that I had help.

At every step of the way I began to identify the human help I received. My parents, my teachers, colleagues, friends, and critics—they all contributed to my personal development. Is any biography a private matter? Can it be shaped single-handedly? Or is the final package a community enterprise, the work of many? This renewed my interest in my biography as well as those of others. Perhaps a closer look, a more penetrating analysis of each significant event, could reveal more precisely the contributions made by others.

This began a journey backward through the course of my own life, inspecting every nuance and detail. In this way I uncovered memories that revealed the individuals who had mingled in every episode of my life.

There were some elements of help I could not pin easily on an actual person. Individuals were involved, to be sure. However, the actions of individuals did not lend themselves to analysis without a leap of faith. Why did someone go out of their way to help me when there seemed no rational reason for them to do so? Why did someone break a well-established pattern to help me, when it would have been easier and more rewarding for him or her to move according to well-formed habit? Why were some events postponed or hastened from their natural course, seemingly for my benefit? In some cases individuals stepped in for a single bit of help and then blended themselves back into their customary pattern as if to be there only for my benefit.

After a few such examples, I began to look for them in all the significant events in my life. In this way I demonstrated to myself the presence of the "invisible hand" throughout my biography. I learned to notice what I had not noticed before. I began to see that special touch in the events. I followed a trail throughout my biography of the footprints of an Angel, the one invisible participant in my story. I wanted to leave behind a record of what I did and what she did.

Hence this little book!

Many of us can't even acknowledge the existence of the angel. Many long to accept the presence of their individual angels, but only as a belief that is vague and composed mostly of wishful thinking. So few of us have direct experience of our angel and almost none of us have figured out how the angel plays into life and what is the most healthy, ethical relationship with this invisible being.

Many of us will find that our lives will begin to seem incomprehensible unless we acknowledge this relationship. Many more people during the next years and beyond will openly describe what they are experiencing as a result of their connection with the angel.

I am of the mind that we humans are changing incredibly rapidly and that the most significant change will be that the term "spiritual" will become more definitive and will mean "angel." The path to spirit is by way of the angel. When most of us speak about God, we are really talking about the angel, our only actual route to all the non-human spirituality of the universe.

This book is divided into (1) **Episodes, or life stories, that illustrate joint angel/human happenings;** (2) Comments exploring the possible insights to be gained from the episodes; and (3) *Conclusions about angel behavior as distinct from human behavior.*

I do not believe angels have any gender. That is a peculiarity limited to animals and humans at the present time. However, in order to refer to an angel some pronoun had to be utilized. In order to shock people into wakefulness, I decided to use she and her in reference to my Angel. The reader would be wise not to attach any significance to such use than simply the necessity of language.

Perhaps just one more note as a comment on the search for the individual angel we live with. The access to the angel is automatically denied to many of us because we are missing a certain step in our development. As long as we do not recognize who we really are, the angel must remain hidden. Only those who recognize themselves as spiritual beings—as living temporarily in a material body to unfold as yet mostly unknown and rarely developed capacities—have the prerequisite for finding their angelic companions.

In order to study the interventions of an angel in biography, I use my own story as the one in which I can uncover the host of necessary details. They say the devil is in the details; so is the angel!

SECTION ONE

"The angel does not deal with space, only time. Time is as far down from duration as an angel can penetrate. Therefore the footprints of all angels resemble bookmarks and can only be found in every single biography and in the cumulative story of mankind, the multitude of human biographies we know as history."

I

Episode 1: First Encounter

I was only 7 or perhaps 8 when I was sent to a little family camp together with my two cousins. About two dozen children in all suffered through the ordeal that was supposed to be "good" for us.

I was not used to being away from my mother and became a reluctant camper from day one. A favorite activity of the counselors was a game that favored size, strength and boldness. For some reason it had to be played every day after rest period. By the third day there was no longer any doubt in my mind that it was not my kind of game!

When I found myself at the edge of some tall bushes bordering the yard being used as a playing field, I watched for an opportunity to blend into them and so gradually disappear among them. I considered myself safely invisible and backed deeper and deeper into the underbrush. When I came to a broken fence and noticed the break in it, I wandered a little further and deeper. When I stumbled on a path, I followed that until the voices of the other children and the counselors gradually disappeared. I had gone too far when I noticed the path under my feet had vanished. I threaded my way through the underbrush, between bushes and trees, no longer sure neither where I was nor how I had arrived. I was lost.

The game was a thing of the past; no distant voices to give me direction. I looked around and could not see anything familiar or friendly. Something tugged at my throat and tears welled up and spilled down my face. It felt like all was lost and I would never again be found. It was not my way to scream or call out. I simply suffered, alone! In silent terror I stood rooted to the ground.

"What have we here?" the voice came from behind me.

I turned to look. There was a lady police officer looking at me out of soft brown eyes. She had a kind expression on her face; a gentle smile warmed her features. I felt immediately a little better.

"Do you have a name?" she asked.

"Siegfried," I answered her.

"Siegfried? Well, Siegfried, are you good with dogs?"

"Maybe. A little." I answered truthfully.

"To tell you the truth I am not much good with stray dogs either. Where are you from?"

"I don't know. Over there." I waved my arm vaguely around me.

"Are you from the family group with all the children on Sycamore Street?"

I nodded even though I wasn't sure. It seemed like the right thing to do.

"Here," she said. "Take my hand and let's find out."

No fear, feeling absolutely safe and secure, I walked along with her feeling certain that all was going to be right with the world. That wonderful feeling, which I have had so often in my later life, took over and I cheerfully moved along without a worry in the world. I was in good hands.

I never saw that police officer again after she delivered me. My memory of her is a little hazy, but my feelings before and after she found me are indelible. The terror of being completely alone and lost before the sound of her voice can never be forgotten. The immense comfort and security charging me through her hand is still alive in me.

Is it possible I had made the first contact with an angel?

2

Commentary on Space

All I knew at the time was that I went from a condition of terror to a condition of safety and that something in the event must have brought about the change. At the time I just accepted the change gratefully and had no great concern with what caused it.

It was quite natural to allocate the change to the person of the police officer. She was such a pleasant person; it was easy to be grateful to her for my rescue. At first I didn't really notice all the details, nor did I notice my feelings as they matured through the event. As I recalled the event in later years, a number of questions assailed me.

The police officer seemed to appear out of nowhere. I didn't hear her crashing through the underbrush or shouting to me from a distance. She appeared soundlessly out of nowhere, as I recall. I accepted her appearance without question. I associated her appearance with the change in my condition, although it wasn't till she took my hand that the full import of my improved situation came home to me.

I could have asked why was she there? Was she there for my sake or did she have another purpose? Did her reason for being there have something to do with the dog she mentioned? Did someone complain about my crying or maybe about a dog? I just did not know everything that went on behind the scenes leading up to the moment she appeared and rescued me.

Looking back on the event, I have a different perspective, an inquiring one. Was it some kind of miracle that she appeared in the space behind me? I am blind to what happens behind me so I couldn't know for sure what brought her into my vicinity.

Since she appeared from behind me, questions begin to arise about our relationship to space. We seem to be formed in such a way that we are vulnerable to space behind us. Our faces look forward. Our eyes see straight ahead with a little peripheral sensitivity. We generally know what is ahead of us in space. What is behind us in space is unknown, unless we turn to look. Our spatial vulnerability is located at our back. She had come to me out of the unknown at my back.

In time we are organized differently. We know what has happened yesterday, last week and even years ago. We are so organized that yesterday is a clear experience, but do we know what is ahead of us in time? Not at all! We can only look backward in time through the organs in us connected with memory. We have no idea what will be happening the next moment in time.

Once I was driving north on a highway when I saw the most terrible accident in the opposite lanes going south. Everyone slowed down out of shock and also a morbid interest in the tragedy on the other side of the median.

A little later after I had passed all the cars stopped in all the opposite lanes going south, the traffic began to thin and cars were moving slowly as they approached the accident area. Even further along north, the cars were moving quite freely; they had no idea of the accident they were moving toward. Still further I saw a convertible with its top down, a man and a woman in the front seat and two children in the back. I noticed their smiling faces and fragments of their singing came through my open window.

That's when I realized, "They don't know what's ahead! They have no idea of the pile up down the road and that they will soon have to come to a screeching halt and take their place in two miles of standstill traffic!"

Their happiness and joy, singing their way into the unknown, began to have new meaning for me. Do we ever, ever know what is ahead of us? Are we actually, in time, at the brink of a precipice? Is the unknown in time invisible to us at every moment and we mask it by projecting across the precipice our plans and intentions? Do we look straightforward in space and delude ourselves that we know what is coming to meet us in time? Our time vulnerability is constantly before us.

We imagine how much better we could organize our lives if we only knew what was about to meet us in time. We think we could prepare ourselves if we knew. Maybe we could take an alternate route. We could stock up on flashlights, water and food, if we only knew. We could save our profits if we knew about the losses of tomorrow; we might even prevent them, if we only knew.

Of course, if we really knew what was ahead of us, we might never commit ourselves to any relationship. We might never start a new business. We might never form a partnership with someone else. We might never have any children if we really knew what it was like to get up in the night for feeding, what it meant to be by their sides in illnesses and accidents, to painfully cooperate in their struggle to become adults. Maybe it is better after all that we are shielded from the reality in time. Maybe we are not yet strong enough to endure consciously what we must go through to create a biography.

We seem to be very solidly imbedded in space. All our senses are organized to deal with space and matter. However, the appearance of the police officer was so timely, so just right it suggests that someone was operating fully aware of the time. Another consciousness than mine was active, one that was aware of time. Perhaps such a consciousness is imbedded more deeply in time but not so much in space. Could I be the one moving in space, more or less unaware of time, while this other consciousness, operating out of a time experience that cannot deal with space except through me, is fully at home in time?

Perhaps the awareness of time more as a total continuum—of future and past while consciously connected with the present moment as the time keyhole through which the past and future are visible—has an influence over me.

Is it possible that such an invisible being, unable to function in space, knows my whole life in its architecture, permits involvement as we together move in time? I would be vulnerable to the future, this other non-material being vulnerable to what I do in space.

In need of a name, I decided to call this being my Angel. She would know the other half of my biography and between the two of us live it out in reality. We would be vulnerable to each other, partners in development, I never knowing what would come to meet me in time, she never knowing how I would respond to what approached me as necessity in space.

Perhaps I needed to know this angel well to work collaboratively. As long as I thought I was in charge and only I was involved in a lifetime, any such collaboration was not impossible, but certainly unconscious. Did I want to go through life ignoring any interventions I could not explain?

I look back over my life and conclude that there is such a being that seems to know all that I do not know. I live and will my half, which she would have to accept. The two halves become a single biography.

If there is such a being, my Angel, then how can I be sure, how can I come to know her, and how can I discover where to look for her involvement. I came to the conclusion that the best possible place to find her was in my life story, my biography. That's why I cannot describe more about my Angel without looking further into my biography, which we seem to own jointly.

3

First Conclusions about Angel Behavior

So how do I keep from fooling myself? Just because she was a nice police officer and I was desperate does not make her an angel. It helps to look back on the event. I may be distorting it slightly from the perspective of seventy years later, but on the other hand I am not so directly involved and can try to be more objective.

I just can't believe that the police officer in my early experience was an angel. Could she have been a mirage? But I know she was real, because I had my hand in hers? A mirage does not suddenly have a real hand to hold. It was warm, firm and human. No doubt about that! The police officer was a human being, not an angel!

There is no denying the absolute confidence, trust and feeling of safety I had. It is still as real in my memory as it was then. I knew without a doubt that I was in safe hands even though I was generally wary of strangers. I also had not had any prior experience with police that I could remember, but it is possible that I attached impressions of safety to the idea of a police officer. I could not rule that out.

Thoroughly investigating my memory, I discovered that my feelings of security did not begin solely with the person of the police officer. It was the whole situation and how it had developed that gave me peace and trust. The event felt well managed. It was the total context of my situation that gave me the feeling I was being protected and cared for. It was her appearance out of nowhere, her friendly eyes, her manner of speaking, her apparent understanding of the whole situation. How had she become what she was to me? How had she ended up in the right place at the right time for me? How did she know what to say, what tone of voice to use?

I never learned all that had gone on before she appeared behind me and spoke. For all I know this was not her regular beat. Perhaps the officer usually on duty called in sick or was required elsewhere. Perhaps this officer was around when the call came in about a stray coyote or dog and she said, "I'll go." She probably wondered why she volunteered so readily, as she was not a dog person or perhaps didn't even know the area from which the call was made. She felt it was her call? Why? Who knows!

That's another thing! Who did make that call? If she or he had made such a call many times before, the police would probably not have responded with a live officer. No, this was a special call to elicit such prompt response. Also, why only one officer? If it were a squad car, then there would have been two officers. The officer took me by the hand and walked me through the woods and to the front of the property on Sycamore Street. She must have been in the neighborhood for another matter, already positioned as it were for my rescue.

There was about the whole event something a little mysterious, something delicately organized in the movements of all those involved. At the time I took it pretty much for granted, but now looking back I am confident the so-called "invisible hand" in the event was palpable. If nothing like that ever happened again, I would certainly have chalked it up to a whole network of coincidences and left it at that.

But my whole life is stacked with such events, each revealing subtle differences and nuances from which I gradually acquired an *intimate knowledge of my Angel. I have never "seen" my Angel. I can't prove her existence to anyone else. I can only know of her effects in the course of my life. In this instance she protected me and left as a residue an all-abiding confidence in life. No matter what happened to me I had absolute certainty that I would never be completely alone. No matter what will happen to me in the future I move in surety that my invisible twin suffers and succeeds with me, I in space, she in time.*

So looking back on this early first encounter with my Angel, I acquire a few fragments of knowledge about her behavior, what she can do and not do. First of all, she is not in a body. If that is so, I will never see her with the same eyes I now have for viewing the world.

It seems she can approach me through a network of interlocking influences that seem to choreograph the movements of others so that just the right outcome surrounds me or confronts me out of time to protect me in space. That's the closest I can get to understanding her involvement in my life from this first encounter as a child.

Now, if my Angel actually does not have a physical body, I will never discover her in space. Sometimes the clouds arrange themselves in such a way that I see a face or a form and think I have glimpsed an angel. I love that illusion because it bolsters my faith and gives materialists a chance to laugh at me, which is good because we are all materialists in our time and a good laugh is very healthy.

Should we perhaps see a vision of an angel with our eyes, it would have to be a spiritual being that takes on a physical body. In other words, it would be human. That's what we are! We are spiritual beings that are incorporated in a physical body in order to have an earthly life. An angel does not inhabit a physical body and is therefore not visible to the eyes.

Should we perhaps in a devout moment hear a voice speaking directly to us with considerable import, know that it is not an angel! Angels do not have a larynx with which to form words and generate vibrations in the air. They cannot be seen or heard or perceived with any of our normal senses that are actually organs for perceiving space and matter. To be human beings necessitates being materialists!

If we are looking for proof that angels exist we should not look for them in space where they do not exist. Nor should we expect them to be human. We already have lots of humans to help us and challenge us. Then where should we look for our angel?

The answer is really quite simple. We should look for our angel in our biography, nowhere else.

She also seems to work from behind the scene, not front and center in my life. She leaves effects that reveal her presence in retrospect from behind the scenery and props. I can strain my eyes, but she is not there. She does not move objects around in life. She does not raise or lower the curtain. She does not place objects in front of me to fall over or notice. She can only influence the world through me or through someone else. Her field of activity must be the consciousness of humans, my consciousness. So that when she approaches something in me stirs, premonitions arise, instincts come alive, feelings surface out of the depths, an idea forms in me. In order to influence anything in space she has to influence one of us humans in time.

How do I know this? How do I know it is an angel? Well, at first I do not. I have the illusion that the source of all this is me. As you can guess I think highly of myself. However, tracing back through my memories, I discover I cannot really determine how I brought such feelings, impulses and ideas about. I know how I make a casserole or cook an omelet. I know every step of the way. I cannot find the beginning of an idea, a feeling or an impulse in myself. I only know, "It comes to me."

So, does my Angel also "come to me" and as a result I have an idea or a feeling? Is her coming perceived by me as an idea or a feeling? Not all ideas or feelings are like that, but certain ones seem to have her monograph on them.

Apparently, the angel lives and works with us from behind the scenes of our activity in space. She remains invisible, approaches or distances herself from us, flowing and undulating in time near or far from our consciousness as our intentions, motives and actions call to her. We don't know it is an angel. We only know an idea comes to us out of nowhere, probably from behind, out of time.

I decided to look even more closely at other events in my life. Are there indications, marks and footprints in time to verify her existence? My search for them began.

4

Episode 2: What's Good, What's Bad?

I attended the Rudolf Steiner School in New York City until the end of the fifth grade. My stepfather and my mother owned a rooming/apartment house together. My mother took care of much of the cleaning in the building. My stepfather took care of the business end and the repair and maintenance. I learned a great deal by following him around watching what he did. I had a small stool that I carried about, set it down where he was working, sat on it and watched. Sometimes I was allowed to hand him tools or hold something carefully until he needed it back.

My stepfather was a frustrated artist. When he graduated from high school, he wanted to attend an arts institute to perfect his painting, drawing and piano playing. His father said, "Fine! However, you first get yourself a 'real' degree that you can fall back on in the event you want to eat." So, my stepfather ended up with a mechanical engineering degree.

He never got the chance to see whether his artistic skills could be a career. When he met my mother, they first formed a kind of business partnership and purchased the rooming house and then married as a practical arrangement. My stepfather had a soft spot for artists. Gradually the rooming house filled with artists of one kind or another. I still remember how my stepfather admired the opera singer on the third floor, a trumpet player and a pianist.

Unfortunately, the second wave of the depression in 1939 was not good for artists. Nor was it good for people who rented rooms and efficiency units to artists. My stepfather and mother made do with less and less rent until finally the business and the property had to be abandoned. It was in New York City, Central Park West in the upper sixties, a very fashionable and expensive location today.

My stepfather's engineering degree then came in handy and he accepted a job with Edison Company in East Orange, New Jersey. Until his retirement he worked on a single machine that turned out small batteries by the millions. On the day of his retirement, he had taken it from a room-sized contraption to a fully automatic machine no larger than fit on a dining room–sized table. Every evening when he returned from work, he put a cold compress on his forehead, sat in the dark and dozed until his migraine gradually disappeared. After a light supper, he played the piano and sang Schubert songs "to restore his soul."

My Angel became active and left her telltale marks just as we first moved to New Jersey. I had to leave the Rudolf Steiner School in New York City, my friends and beloved teachers. I could not understand why this was necessary. My mother explained that my stepfather needed a job and had found one, but it was in New Jersey.

"Why couldn't he find one here?"

"He has been looking, but none could give him enough income for all of us to live."

It sounded so completely rational. Both of them looked straight at me as though this reason was completely self-evident and needed no other explanation. As far as I was concerned, it didn't explain anything. It didn't explain why income was more important than close friends and teachers. It didn't explain why everything had to be disrupted just for something called income. However, the sheer

Episode 2: *What's Good, What's Bad?*

weight of their facial expressions and certainty left me speechless and we moved. I thought everything worthwhile had ended and from now on it was a matter of endurance.

I was enrolled in a public school. I was thrown in with ordinary students, most of whom did not know why they were there. Everybody teased and jeered and fought each other in the cement schoolyard. Being punished was a badge of honor everyone aspired to. Within a week I had my first fist fight with a boy who refused to leave me alone, misreading my reticence as cowardice. Eventually I had to set him straight in a very clumsy but determined manner. We were pulled apart and punished. Once punished, I was accepted as a regular person.

Miss Brown was six feet tall, wore a grey wig and knew exactly why she was there. The first day we sat at our desks and she waited for the bell to ring before addressing us in a dry crisp voice.

"Every day when you come into this classroom you will have in your hand a sheet of paper on which you have written your homework assignment for the day. You will march to the front of the room and place your completed assignment on this right hand corner of my desk.

"It may be that there is a day when you have been out raising mischief and forgot to do your homework. If so, DO NOT COME TO SCHOOL! Perhaps you have been up to no good on the way home from school, and your homework was ripped up, lost or otherwise disposed of. If so, DO NOT COME TO SCHOOL. Perhaps you do have to come to school without your homework in hand, for any number of reasons. If so, DO NOT COME TO MY CLASSROOM. GO TO THE OFFICE and present yourself for appropriate action. IS THIS UNDERSTOOD? DOES ANYONE NOT UNDERSTAND WHAT I HAVE JUST SAID?"

Silence in class!

After a moment Miss Brown continued in a more friendly tone. "After you have deposited your homework right there, go to your own desk, take out a sheet of paper and copy your homework assignment for the next day which you will see in the upper right hand corner of the blackboard. Perhaps you are wondering when there might not be an assignment written in that corner signifying that you have no homework for that evening. NEVER! It will always be there as long as you are in my class.

"And do you know what? You will always pass this course if you do what I tell you. Anyone who does his or her homework every evening and turns it in the next morning as I have explained to you WILL PASS THIS COURSE! UNDERSTOOD?"

I ended up on the star honor roll every single report period. I did what she demanded and sure enough it worked. This was a new experience for me. At the Rudolf Steiner School in New York City all my creative capacities were engaged. The academic work was completely integrated with the artistic work. We compiled our own textbooks and made them beautiful so that they could be displayed in prominent places for all to see. The teachers usually presented the material to be learned, engaged us in conversation about it, asked for recall on earlier subjects and encouraged us to express our own thoughts. It was a very creative process and we each learned within the context of a rich life experience. We learned continuously but none of us had any idea if we were passing or not. Actually we assumed we must be OK if we were still in the classroom and not in the office.

In the sixth, seventh and eighth grades I had Miss Schneider, Miss Brownell and Miss Brown, each more rigorous and disciplined than the next. Passing meant doing exactly what you were told to do. It was so simple. It was refreshing, and even restful in the sense that you were never at a loss for what was right or wrong. Life had become an endless string of correct answers.

All right, now where was my Angel while all this was going on? Neither Miss Schneider, nor Miss Brownell nor Miss Brown looked at all like angels. Certainly none of the other students around me were angels. More likely the opposite was true. We were all up to mischief any chance we could get and there were many opportunities. However, the boundaries were all clearly drawn and no doubt ever existed as to what was correct and what was incorrect. Good or bad was removed from the experience of learning and correct and incorrect replaced them.

5

Second Conclusions about Angel Behavior

So where was my Angel? Why am I so grateful to her seventy years later? I was at first so miserable leaving the Rudolf Steiner School in New York City and being forced to live in Orange, New Jersey and attend the public school. At the time if I suspected my Angel was involved in that, I would have thought she was punishing me for having such a good time growing up. In my own dreamy way I was totally immersed in my life at the school.

True, I was in the Rudolf Steiner School office a great deal. I barely remember what was going on in class, but I knew everyone's job in the office. It got so I could direct a visitor properly and point staff to something they were looking for. However, I was dreaming it all. I hadn't come down yet into my body nor was my attention really on academic achievement.

All that changed in the public school in Orange, New Jersey. I emerged from my childhood dream and awoke to the new realities. Only in much later years did I manage to be grateful for that awakening. Schneider, Brownell and Brown gave me discipline, self-awareness and self-respect. I never again confronted anything I couldn't tackle with a little effort. What seemed like a terrible thing at the time turned out to be a godsend! Had I not been torn out of the Rudolf Steiner School, which felt like a really bad thing,

I might never have come under the iron rule of Schneider, Brownell and Brown, which turned out to be a good thing.

How did it all happen? Well, I know a little about that. It seemed that the Principal learned that I had come from a Waldorf type school in New York City. He had heard of that kind of school and respected its curriculum and mission. He arranged to have his best teachers take me on and I thrived.

My parents had to suffer bankruptcy. They had to give up their apartment house in New York City and move into an inexpensive apartment in Orange, New Jersey. My stepfather had to take a job for the sake of "income," suffering migraines every night. All this just so I could spend three years with the best teachers in the public school system of Orange, New Jersey. I happily accepted all their sacrifices without a thought. I learned that what may seem horrible, painful and "the end of the world" can easily turn out to be the best thing that ever happened to me.

It seems that sometimes we appear to be guided for our own good even against our own will. What feels awful may turn out to be beneficial. How something feels may be a disguise for some unknown benefit not to be discovered until much later.

My tentative conclusions are that my Angel doesn't regard place, space or matter as having any sort of enduring reality. We notice how old buildings may one day be torn down and then a new structure takes its place. Although we witness continuous decay and rebuilding around us, we nevertheless have a high degree of confidence that this world and almost everything in it is here to stay.

We see that plants wilt and die over the winter months, but then shoot forth again the following spring. We see the leaves blaze in the autumn, dry to paper and fall to the ground, leaving the trees bare for winter only to sprout anew come spring.

A little later I will be able to tell you how I found out my Angel has a different perspective. Right now, I found out my Angel views the changes in life more like the changes in scenery on the stage than the illusion of permanence in space and matter. When we enjoy a good play, the actors are visible to us and we see them within the context of their scenery. We do not see the stage manager or all the stagehands working behind the scenery. We, the audience, just accept that the new scenery represents a situation that has real existence even though we see only a fragment of it with each scene. The scene changes because the action of the play demands a different place, or even the same place if that is the case.

Just as the actors and the action on a stage move from place to place, we, too, move from place to place in our lives, from space to space, chaining our intended activity to matter and space.

The angel seems to regard all such places in the material world not as fixed or permanent, but more as scenery necessary to human life and human activity. Knowing much of the whole play, the angel works from behind the scenes, while we the actors strut about on our stage, whatever scenery happens to be there.

The angel is never on the stage. She is always in the background, sometimes keenly interested in what is going on because she knows how the future is working on the present and how the past often finds its real meaning in the future. Sometimes we bore her and she withdraws, giving us a hiatus without angel influence. In the end, she has no choice. She is bound with iron necessity to one of us and cannot progress further in her development unless her co-biographer also progresses in whatever way is possible.

What is real and has enduring existence is what we would call relationships. Who we find or lose, love or hate, help or hinder is the stuff of angel reality.

What have I discovered? I concluded that while I move from place to place all day long while I am awake, my Angel influences me to move from person to person.

Her oversight allows me to connect or disconnect from my contemporaries without knowing why. She has the "why" firmly in her grip; I have the "what" and the "where"!

6

Epidode 3: I Find Myself (maybe)

It was in my 12th year of schooling that I first found out where to look for my angel and have a reliable contact point.

I began some serious study in Yoga, not with a teacher, but using a few scraps of information a friend passed on to me. The idea was to sit in the lotus position and undertake some determined meditative practices. I probably should have sought out a master, but at 17 years, one still thinks one can know and do everything. So I just started and kept at it.

I would take the lotus position, relax my shoulders and arms, untie slowly all the knots and hard places in my head and slowly sink into the void. It went well. There were always the random thoughts that crept into my consciousness, but I learned to be ruthless. Even the really good ideas were ousted, which for me was very difficult. When a good idea came, which wasn't that often, I treasured it and would have loved to write it down or retain it somehow. However, with typical single-minded determination I discarded it and returned to the void.

One day something remarkable happened. From the void I experienced myself sitting in the lotus position meditating. I saw the surrounding space where I sat and looked down on myself and knew I had achieved a rare objective view of Siegfried.

More practice and I was able to hold that view for minutes at a time although the awareness of time was not included. Considering that I was about as disconnected from myself as was possible, I nevertheless felt remarkably engaged, as if I was participating in my existence from a new vantage point. All of this was very exciting and I returned again and again.

One late afternoon, I went alone into one of the classrooms at High Mowing School, where I was a boarding student. The weekends were usually quite relaxed. It was a good time to practice one's musical instrument, work on the "good" book record of the main lesson of the block or else take walks or read.

I climbed up on a table in the classroom, which positioned me about 30 inches from the floor in a corner of the classroom and took the lotus position. I had a feeling that today the mood and context of my situation foreboded a new potential step in my meditative practice. I had no idea what awaited me.

It was amazing how quickly I achieved presence in the void and looked down upon myself in meditative condition. I saw the whole classroom, the different tables and chairs, the drawings and writing left over on the blackboards. In slow motion, calmly, deeply peaceful, I surveyed it all in color no less. I was content with my overview of existence.

As I watched from the void with my eyes closed, the door to the classroom opened, two students whom I knew very well entered the classroom, took a table near the door, immediately dropped into chairs and continued an animated discussion about a project they were both undertaking for their physics class.

I observed them, eyes closed, from out of the void, including myself sitting on the table in the corner. Every word they exchanged had layers and layers of meaning. Each time they paused I knew what they were thinking. I even experienced what they were feeling as they met in ideas and emotions swirling about them, drawing them together and pushing them apart in a kind of Technicolor dance. All the time I watched, they were sitting, gesturing and laughing, even disagreeing on issues.

At last, after considerable drama and shifting in attitudes, they came together in agreement and bolted from the room, each set on following up on what they had agreed to do. The door was left open. The classroom lights were still on.

Neither one of the other students had seen me or noticed that I was in the room. They went about their business thinking themselves in complete privacy. For them I did not exist. I had become invisible, removed from the sensory world. I was void.

Something stirred in my consciousness. I was disturbed and found myself falling back into myself, still harboring some feeling of unrest and distress. I sat there on the table, unraveled myself from the lotus position and pondered what was going on in me.

Then I knew. I wanted to be engaged in life. I wanted to be an actor on the stage with other humans. I wanted to make a difference in what was happening on the earth. I felt a deep and irresistible intention to climb into my life and lead it to the fullest. I became determined to experience everything there is to experience by being alive and deeply engaged in whatever life had to offer me.

7

THIRD CONCLUSIONS ABOUT ANGEL BEHAVIOR

It was a turning point in my life. I never practiced my personal version of Yoga again. It left me in a moment, even though it had taken me months to get anywhere with it. It vanished so quickly I barely noticed its departure.

The insight on my own nature and intention toward life was long lasting. Even today I can re-experience that moment of understanding and self-knowledge. What is strange is that I did not struggle for it. It came like a gift. It settled into my awareness like a New Hampshire rain, or perhaps it blossomed effortlessly like laurel on the hillsides around High Mowing School. It was worth my whole education to have had that moment given to me.

Insight comes so unexpectedly. It's always a surprise. It storms in as a display of power and urgency. For those of us who need to be sure and are often skeptical of insight, it sometimes takes hours, days or even weeks to test and verify the truthfulness of an insight, yet throughout this subsequent period there is the nagging feeling that it is probably correct and charges in on us from a source hugely wiser than we are.

Every time it happens to me, sometimes in hindsight, I dig back into the actual internal event of its appearance, tracing each nuance of feeling, observing again the sequence of thoughts that seemed to lure the insightful idea into my consciousness. To this day I have not identified the pattern of ideas and feelings that inevitably bring about insight so that I can repeat the process with an equally reliable result. So now I conclude that each time I need insight or even just better understanding of an issue, I must approach it with something unique to the situation; I must be creative, not analytical.

In other words, I have to generate effort and warmth in me if light is to be shed into the darkness of my search. The simple fact that I search for understanding, not taking any easy answer, always willing to remain creative in the process, affords the best chance of a response from my Angel. Sometimes I can actually feel her being drawn toward me and into my life if I can just fill myself with the right ingredients, consisting mostly of warmth, a kind of focused energy, openness of mind and patience.

I have so far learned quite a bit about my Angel and might sum it up as follows:

1. *Just as I have to follow certain laws simply because I am in a body and must function in space, so my Angel seems to be subject to certain rules and restrictions in order to function in time.*
2. *Maybe your angel is different, but mine does not seem to have a planned agenda nor does she make rational decisions the way we think we do. She seems to follow my lead up to a point. She simply draws near me either from the future or from the past and, in so doing, her very proximity affects my feelings and thoughts. I experience her attention on me as a feeling or thought. They are the thoughts I am usually most inclined to implement with very little screening or filtering.*

3. *Although every single sense impression arouses feelings of one kind or another in me, the feelings that indicate the interest of my Angel appear "out of nowhere." They apparently are not attached to any particular sense impression or sensation. Hence they have a certain mystery about them. The stimulus for such feelings and thoughts is not in this special world of mine. They come to me from outside it.*

4. *My Angel is not forefront on the stage the way I am. She lives behind the scenery that I take for reality and never shows herself except as an idea or feeling. There is no way any of us will experience our angels unless we accept our feelings and thoughts as realities. A feeling and a thought must be as real as a banana or a laptop if we are to experience the attentions of our angels as anything but accidental or coincidental occurrences.*

5. *It appears my Angel is not in a physical body, does not need one nor desire one. Her influence on me is neither direct nor focused. She does not approach me from within another person. She simply approaches and influences the entire network of factors operating in my space at that moment in time. In other words, my Angel is not the police officer.*

6. *The angel cannot deal with space, only time. Time is as far down from duration as an angel can penetrate. Therefore the footprints of all angels can only be found in the cumulative story of mankind, the multitude of human biographies known as history.*

SECTION TWO

MY ANGEL TURNS ME LOOSE

"We die and are born again, entangled in the web of relationships we created in the past together with our soul collaborators. Our erstwhile colleagues are all around us."

8

Episode 4: On My Own

I joined two of my high school friends and traveled with them in a black Model A from Wilton, New Hampshire as far as Billings, Montana. Believing my attention was elsewhere, my two friends then huddled off to one side deep in whispered discussion and then they confronted me with the result.

"We are not going any further!" they announced.

"I am not going back until I reach the Pacific Ocean," was my answer.

"How are you going to do that?" they demanded to know. "It's our car."

The next morning they started back. No hard feelings! They are still close friends today. It's just they had enough. I didn't.

I found the yard where they were knocking freight trains together. A few hobos were sitting together eating soup out of cans. From them I learned the ropes.

"Don't get on until it starts to move."

"Watch out for the railroad dicks. They'll knock you off with clubs."

"Keep go'n west. Aim for Yakama! They'll be pick'n apricots, early peaches, cherries. A few days work, at least."

"Once you're in a reefer, the dicks will leave you alone. They know better than to follow you into a reefer."

"All the reefers will be going west empty and load ice and fruit in Yakama. Aim for the ice compartment at the end of the reefer, but get up there fast before you get caught."

I waited near the tracks and watched the different strings of cars. Eventually one of the hobos told me which train looked almost put together for the trip west. I waited ages for it to move.

Once I heard a scream and I could hear many bodies hurrying into the brush away from the tracks. I guessed some poor fellow got caught and thanked my stars it wasn't me.

From the creaking sounds along the train I guessed it was about to move and sure enough, it started to inch forward. I waited until I was opposite a reefer and ran to climb the iron rungs leading up to the top of the ice compartment. I slipped through one of the trap doors at the top and closed it behind me. It was black inside. Not a glimmer of light anywhere. I felt around me. My fingers hooked into the meshing that enclosed the compartment and I slowly slid down and sat hunched on the floor.

My fingers were sticky. I wiped them on my Levis. Suddenly I heard a noise inside the compartment. It was a kind of sucking noise, a bit like a cork popping out of a bottle. I didn't move. Again the same noise! I waited and kept quiet. The same noise was repeated every three or four minutes.

"Howdy." The voice sounded from inside the compartment. Then the cork noise again.

"Howdy," I answered.

"Goin' west?"

"Yeah,"

Silence! There were three of us in that compartment. We traveled all the way to Yakama. They were experienced. They traveled the circuit—apples in New England, tobacco in the Carolinas, peaches in Georgia, then oranges, grapefruit and lemons in Florida, sugar beets, cabbages, carrots all through the south. Who knows where else, but now it was time to be in Yakama.

Every now and then one of them would spit tobacco juice into the metal netting with that familiar cork-popping sound. Out of consideration he learned not to aim it anywhere near the sound of my voice.

During the two days we were in that compartment, we slept, told stories and slept. I did not say much, but I was a good listener. The stories were all pretty much the same; at least they covered the same general theme and its variations.

They entailed meeting a woman who was alone, very fine looking and saucy. Sooner or later, she would suggest he move in with her, as she had a cabin all to herself. "Oh, oh," said the other man; "Look out!" Well, it turns out he resisted her entreaties for quite some time, but finally, out of sympathy or because he felt sorry for her, he would agree. "It happens all the time," the other man would join in.

Everything went along beautifully until his first pay. Then all of a sudden it seemed he owed her something and the virtue of sharing everything was extolled. "Yeah, we know how that ends up." The other man would chime in.

"Well, out of the kindness of my heart I give her some of my money. At first she seems satisfied with that, but then one day she asks me to get some sticks for the stove or even to fetch some water from the well. Every day it gets worse and worse. You know, I barely escaped in time. Another few days and I would have been trapped for good, lock, stock and barrel!"

"Man, ain't that the truth! Let me tell you how I just barely escaped with my life in Texas last year," the other man commiserated and began to tell his story that was pretty much the same theme.

Every story always involved getting trapped into staying in the same place, saddled with obligations and rules, and most important, a narrow escape into freedom and travel. I listened to all of them and in the course of the next few months was astounded to hear the same theme again and again in Washington, Oregon and California, whenever I was lucky enough to sit down with itinerant workers on the loose.

I did not stay in Yakima, not even for one day. I was determined to get to the Pacific Ocean. The next freight train I caught had mostly flatcars and cattle cars being pulled empty to the coast. I jumped an empty cattle car. I loved the animal smell, but it tended to stick with me the longer I traveled in it.

9

Episode 5: Selling Religion

I arrived in Seattle, Washington, early in July 1950, with one dollar in my pocket. The question was what to do with one dollar. Even in those days a dollar did not go far. I purchased the largest bottle of Gallo wine I had ever seen, drank it slowly and happily and, feeling no pain, slept the night in skid row near the waterfront. In those days, it was and unsavory resting place.

The next morning my head ached, I smelled really bad and looked even worse in my old Levis, dirty shirt and peeling sneakers. I also no longer had a dollar bill in my pocket, which should not have surprised me. I knew I needed to find some work. As I walked about in Seattle, I passed an office building whose name I cannot recall. In front of it was a parked car and two men were standing by its open door talking about religious matters as far as I could understand. The Bible was mentioned several times.

"Either of you gentlemen happen to know where I could find some work?" I asked them hopefully.

They glanced at each other briefly. I thought I caught a look of amusement that was quickly suppressed. One of the men smiled at me.

"Look, if you go up to the 12th floor, room 1209, you will run into Mr. Barrett. Maybe he could give you a job selling Bibles."

"Thanks."

From the lobby I approached the elevator before I noticed people staring at me and skirting around my whereabouts. I realized the smell of cattle and manure was probably still on me and I had not washed or shaved for more than a week. My stomach growling forced me to continue.

I had all kinds of space to myself on the crowded elevator and escaped on the 12th floor, to the relief of all the other passengers, I am sure.

Mr. Barrett stared at me and marveled at my guts.

"What makes you think you can sell Bibles?"

"Well, I know a little about the Bible, and I studied yoga for a while. I graduated from High Mowing School, a college prep school in New Hampshire, and I have the feeling I could do almost anything I put my mind to."

"I am glad you know only a little about the Bible. Too much knowledge will just get you into trouble when you're selling. Getting into an argument about religion is the best way to lose a sale."

"Did I mention that I am a fast learner?"

"God help us!" he laughed. He reached into his pocket and gave me $20. "If you still want to join us, be back here in front of the building at 11:00 a.m. sharp dressed in a decent pair of slacks, a tie and shirt and a sport jacket."

"Do I need to have my own Bible?"

"No. I'll take care of that! And by the way, you have to take my training program!"

"Oh, oh," I thought, but it seems I also must have said it.

"Is there something wrong with that?"

"No, no. It's just that I need to start earning enough to eat pretty soon."

"No problem! My training program is only five minutes long, but woe to you if you don't listen."

"Oh, I'll listen real good!"

That's how I landed a job selling Bibles all over the place in the states of Washington and Oregon. I returned to skid row, found a pawn shop and, believe it or not, bought a pair of slacks, a shirt and tie, a pair of shoes and a sport jacket for $17. I was hungry and ready to start at 11:00 a.m.

You may be wondering how my Angel fits into this story. Perhaps she doesn't. No doubt you thought I was one of those people who blame everything that goes wrong on the devil and everything that happens to go well on my Angel. Maybe you thought I pray fervently to my Angel for advice on whether to eat broccoli or macaroni and cheese. That's not me. I am a very independent sort of fellow and take responsibility for all my own actions and mistakes. My Angel is a reality and I will not cheapen her existence with superstitious beliefs. It is the height of arrogance to think that angels have nothing else to do but cater to our every whim and concern.

Episode 6: The Facts of Life

At 11:00 a.m., Mr. Barrett met me in front of the office building, guided me over to a bench, sat down and began his training program.

"There are only three lessons you have to learn. If you learn them and do them you will be a success. Now listen closely!

"You must call on two hundred potential customers every day. By customer I mean a person or household having the potential for buying a Bible. Do you understand me?"

"Sure, I get it."

"Oh man! I was afraid of that. You are not listening to me."

"Yes, I am! Two hundred customers every day! I understand." I wasn't stupid and knew exactly what he said.

"Oh well! I tried. Now you'll just have to learn the hard way." He shook his head sadly.

"I really did hear every word you said and believe it or not I will call on two hundred customers each day."

"Well, we'll see!" he glared at me. "The second rule is never be discouraged by what you see before, during and after your sales call. Take in all the details, but do not let it deter you from making the sales call. You might see a frightful mess on the porch or hear babies screaming or crying inside the house. Don't let it stop you from making the call. Once, a woman with two screaming kids bought my Bible just to get rid of me. Get it?"

"Yes, I get it."

"My third rule is this. No matter how kind, friendly the customers may be or how interested they are in you or the Bible, once they start talking about its contents, turn around and leave. Once the subject of religion comes up, LEAVE! Otherwise you will be there an hour and a half and still not sell a Bible. Nobody who is really deeply interested in religion will buy it from you. They just want to talk with you about it. They probably already have one and have studied it for years and want to convert you. So turn around and get out even if you have to be rude."

"Great! Thank you. What else?"

"That's it!"

"That's it?"

"That's it!"

We rose and made our way to the waiting car. The same two men I had seen earlier were standing by. Two women were seated in the car. The man who had given me the suggestion to go up in the office building and see Mr. Barrett grinned.

By way of an apology, he said, "I see you got the job. You look a lot better than you did earlier."

"Thank you, I appreciate this chance to work."

Mr. Barrett introduced me to Gerald and his wife Lucy. Thor and Belinda introduced themselves in friendly fashion. We all climbed into the car and drove off.

Gerald was the boss. He kept the Bibles in the trunk of his car. He sold the Bibles to us for $12 and we sold them to customers for $20. He did not seem to care how much we charged for them as long as we paid him $12 for each. I always assumed he paid $12 to

Mr. Barrett for each, but in hindsight I imagine he bought them from Mr. Barrett for $10. After all, it was his car and someone had to pay for service and gasoline.

There was a more expensive Bible that we could buy for $15 and sell for $25. Gerald seemed to like them and sold a few, but the rest of us preferred the $20 Bible. Each of us carried two or three in a briefcase.

Gerald always wore a hat, a light blue suit and black shoes. Lucy wore bobby socks, short skirts and brown and white pumps. She had her hair in pigtails and chewed bubble gum continuously. I remember being introduced to her as Lucy, but I only heard her called Sweetie by Gerald, and neither Thor nor Belinda every spoke with her. I followed suit and never spoke to her either. Every now and then she craved something and pestered Gerald without mercy. He hardly ever gave in.

"Now Sweetie," he soothed. "You know you don't need that and can manage very well without it. Daddy will get something special when we next stop."

She pouted for a while and then cuddled up to him in the front seat with a resigned sigh.

I first thought maybe she was his daughter, but every now and then, turning sideways, I noticed she seemed a bit older and gradually I understood she was his wife. At any rate whenever we stopped for the night, they both disappeared rapidly into their motel room and were not seen again until morning.

Thor was short and stocky, with black hair and a swarthy complexion. His name suggested a Scandinavian descent but he never spoke of it. Belinda always sat next to him. She was the one who most often conversed with me. She was interested in my studies, my life, where I had gone to school and my plans for the future.

Whenever we stopped at a motel, she would busy herself with postcards and knickknacks in the office while Thor rented a room. I sometimes caught her quickly disappearing into his room for the night. They were so discreet. She didn't want me to know they slept together, because I was so young and might think badly of her.

We spent the night just outside of a town in the least expensive motel. Gerald knew them all and had planned each stop well. On instructions from Mr. Barrett, he advanced me enough money, which I paid back as soon as possible.

The first morning, Gerald dropped me off with my briefcase of Bibles and papers at the corner of the area I was to penetrate. They drove on. I looked around and began to think of my opening comments. There was a coffee shop right across the street. I stopped there, sat in a booth and looked at my Bible, drinking a cup of coffee. I looked at all the features of this Bible. It had a few pictures, an index, the Old Testament and New Testament, and a family records section. As I glanced through it, I ran into a passage that seemed to prophesy the invention of the car. That might come in handy.

I planned my first few words and sorted through a few contingencies, packed up my briefcase and headed for the door. It had started to rain. Just a shower but I did not want to get my jacket wet so I waited. I ordered another cup of coffee and watched the rain stream off the edge of the roof and splash against the picture window.

At last it slowed to a drizzle and then stopped. The sun shone through and the streets exhaled steam. As I left the coffee shop I looked at my watch. It was 11:25 a.m. How was I ever going to squeeze 200 house calls into the rest of the day? I clamped my jaw down and promised myself to do it.

I finished my last call at 10:00 p.m. that evening. I had done it. I had called on two hundred houses and sold one Bible for cash. I owed Gerald $12, but $8 belonged to me. I was going to eat after all.

We traveled from village to town to city all through Washington and Oregon. Each time we arrived, Gerald would apportion a section of town to each of us. Sometimes, we covered everything in one day; sometimes it took longer. In the next six weeks I sold 71 Bibles. Each sale had a story connected with it.

I learned more about people than I later learned in all my psychology courses in college. Maybe these experiences had more to do with the story of my life than I thought at the time. Perhaps every bit of learning gave meaning to a later episode.

Therefore I mention a few of special interest before my very last memorable sale.

Episode 7: Human Nature

About halfway down the block, I almost turned into a small cottage when I noticed its appearance. The white paint was peeling from it in sheets. The shutters by the side of the two front windows were hanging from single hinges. All the curtains hung in tatters, and pretended to be closed. The lawn consisted of waist-high weeds and empty bottles and cans glinted from underneath the growth. Weeds pushed up between the broken concrete slabs leading to the weathered front door. I thought this was a hopeless case and started to pass it by when I remembered what Mr. Barrett had included in his training.

"No matter what you see, don't let it stop you from making the sales call."

I sighed and reluctantly made my way to the front door. It really looked and felt deserted. I knocked. Nothing happened. I knocked much harder. The sound seemed to echo inside and I thought perhaps it really was deserted and empty.

Then I heard what sounded like a scratching sound or something being dragged across the floor or down a wall. After some more silence I knocked again, this time with my fist. For some inexplicable reason I was becoming annoyed.

I heard the rattling of chains and locks. The door opened a crack. Two beady black eyes peered out at me.

I spoke quickly, explaining that I was calling on all the Christian families in the area to show them the exciting new Bible that had just been published with all sorts of special features. She mumbled something about not being interested.

"When you see it for yourself and have it in your hand you will be interested," I assured her.

"I have a Bible," she said.

"Not one like this."

"I have that one exactly," she insisted and began closing the door.

For some reason I could not fathom, I was irritated with the tone of her voice and pushed against the door to keep it from closing. We ended up both pushing against it and in the tug of war that followed, she suddenly gave way and I almost fell into the house. She had turned away and was walking toward an old sofa at 90 degrees to a bookcase. There was no other furniture in the room. No pictures hung on the walls. Each institutional gray wall glared menacingly at me and offered no promise or comfort.

I followed her into the room and sat down on the opposite end of the sofa. There was no other chair or seating possibility in the room except the sofa. As a matter of fact, there was absolutely nothing to break up the flat floor, walls and ceiling. It was depressing!

I opened my briefcase and removed the Bible halfheartedly.

"Now you say you already have this Bible?"

"Yes."

"I can't see how that's possible. This is brand new, just published."

"Oh, I have it all right!"

"Does it have an index in the back and a page to record your family lineage?"

"Yes."

"This Bible even has a section for looking up various things. For example you might want to find out where the Bible prophesied the automobile. I'm sure the Bible you have doesn't include that!" I challenged her triumphantly.

"It certainly does!" she insisted

"But that's impossible!"

"Well, it does and that's a fact." Her chin jutted out and she was a bundle of indignation. Her two fists were balled tightly in her lap and she glared at me.

I probably should have left it at that, but some instinct kept me pushing.

"What Bible is it that you say has all these features? I'd like to see it."

"You can take my word that I have it right on my shelf where I look at it every day."

"That shelf?" I asked, pointing to the bookcase beside the sofa where she sat.

"Yes!"

I looked at the bookcase and the shelf beside her. For a moment I couldn't believe my eyes. The entire shelf was end-to-end Bibles. So was the shelf above it and the one below it as well. From my quick glance at the three rows, I could not see any that resembled in appearance the Bible I was offering. I decided I would give it one more try in what seemed like a pretty hopeless possibility for a sale.

"Which one is it that is like the one I am offering? I don't see any that resembles this one," I asked.

"It's that one over on the right," she insisted.

I rose from the sofa and reached over to the bookshelf. "This one?" I asked, reaching for one on the right that had a dark blue cover somewhat like the one I was offering her.

She jumped up out of the sofa, grabbed my arm to keep me from pulling it out. There ensued a tussle as I tried to get the Bible out to look inside and she jerked at my arm to keep me from pulling the Bible out of the shelf.

As I finally had the Bible halfway out, she yanked at my arm again and a shower of $20 bills fell to the floor. We were both motionless. I was stunned by the quantity of bills that formed a pile on the floor. She was crestfallen, meekly easing back into the sofa, lowering her head and clenching her hands together.

For a moment I didn't know what to say or do. Then I realized there was nothing to say. I picked up one of the $20 bills and put it in my pocket. I put the Bible in her lap and she seemed to accept it almost gratefully. Then I left.

I tell this story not so much out of joy that I made a sale, or to prove that Mr. Barrett was correct in his advice to me. I tell it as an example of the many different experiences I had going from house to house, each time not knowing what I would encounter and each time amazed at what would greet me from the human beings I had to deal with. At the end of every day I had to have absolute quiet for a few minutes just to digest what I had witnessed that day.

I learned not to have any expectations, and I learned to be totally open to the uniqueness of every single person that seemed to be especially revealed during a buying and selling transaction. It was apparently the type of transaction that opened Pandora's box and released all the desires, foibles, idiosyncrasies and challenges imbedded in being an individual human.

I acquired a store of experiences and adjusted to a wide range of emotions and surprises. I learned to read sign, not the way our ancestors read sign in the early wilderness expanses of this country, but sign that gave me clues as to the nature of the person in the house I was approaching. Every little nuance and detail started to speak to me. If the grass was short, neatly clipped at the edges, I took note. This person had something very precise and orderly about them. If the flower beds were full of blossoms and different varieties of flowers but clogged with weeds, I knew this person cared about their garden but either did not have time to love it or else was a person with good intentions that then faded over time as other matters became serious.

I even got to the point that I noticed the next house in conjunction with the one I was approaching to ferret out clues about their relationship, which I could sometimes use during the sale.

"Too bad your neighbor can't keep their lawn as beautifully as you do!" or "How nice that you find the time to weed a bit of your neighbor's part of the flower bed."

I always stirred up some feelings that helped me to make the person feel good and more inclined to listen to me. I also was then armed with additional information for when I would then call on the house next door.

I discovered that people generally belonged to their space. The way Thurber noticed how dogs and their owners had a certain commonality in their appearance and behavior, so did I see that each person was synchronized with their immediate space. It was as if the surrounding space was an extension of their nature. Humans seemed inclined to adapt their surroundings to fit their characters. As a result, the whole earth was being transformed from its natural state to one that imitated or mimicked the soul characteristics of human beings. Would the world eventually replace the natural order with human nature? Selling Bibles from door to door instilled in me a philosophy of change based on how we humans are changing the world appearance and giving it human characteristics.

Episode 8: Just a Joke

July passed in a blur of villages and towns. We moved out of Washington and into Oregon. In early August one day Gerald decided that by noon we should move on to the next town. He collected us all in the car and we drove out of town. It was a warm day. In the back seat it was even warmer. Holding my sport jacket and briefcase in my lap, I dozed and then slept.

Suddenly the car jerked to a stop.

"This is your sector for the afternoon!" they all shouted at me, pushing the door open and piling everything into my arms. I stumbled out of the car. The door was closed from the inside and they tooted off. I thought I heard laughter from inside the car as I sleepily assembled my thoughts and looked around.

I was on a country road. I looked as far right as possible and then as far left as possible. There was not a house in sight. They had obviously sprung a joke on me and taken advantage of my sleeping in the car. I guess it served me right.

On the other side of the road were already mowed hay fields stretching far in every direction and separated only by barbed wire fences. I guessed that cows or cattle would be let into the fields after most of the hay had been harvested.

On my side of the road were orchards. They looked like peach trees or maybe apricots. There were also a few early apples in large, older trees. I heard voices coming from the trees. Then I noticed the tractor and the collector boxes spaced evenly along the trees. A stack of baskets had fallen over by the tractor.

I slid down the embankment and slowly approached the apple trees.

"Anybody there?" I called up.

"Yo. What's up?"

I tried a little humor. "It looks like you're up, and I'm down here." I was answered by a low chuckle.

"You lost?"

"Nah. My friends dumped me out of the car with a few of the Bibles I'm selling. It was supposed to be a joke, I guess. But I told them just because they're farmers and up in the trees doesn't mean they can't read the Good Book. So here I am."

"You selling Bibles?"

"Yeah."

"Let's have a look."

A basket on the end of a rope came gliding down from above. I put one of the Bibles in the basket and it disappeared up the tree. I picked up a fallen apple and munched on it while I waited.

"How much?"

"Twenty bucks. They're complete, not abridged and the latest features."

The basket came down again. My Bible was inside and with it a $20 bill.

"Can you put the Bible over there on the seat of the tractor? I'll get it later."

"Hey Joel, who you talk'n to?" The voice came from a tree down the row a bit.

"A guy sell'n Bibles."

The other fellow laughed. "You buy one? It ain't gonna get you to heaven, you know, unless you change your ways!" More laughter out of the tops of trees.

"It didn't do me much good either, but the girls sure favor me since I started quoting a few passages," I volunteered. More laughter rumbled from a few other trees.

"Maybe you should take a look for yourself," said the man in the tree above me.

"Let's see." A basket came gliding down two trees along the row.

After about a half hour, a car drove up and started honking its horn. I recognized my team of jokers and climbed up the embankment. They opened the door, laughing.

"Sell any Bibles to the cows?" they all laughed uproariously.

"Why did you come back so soon? I was just getting going. Doing great, as a matter of fact."

"How many?" they demanded, laughing.

I took out the $20 bills and pretended to count them.

"Four! Not bad for a half hour's work and me being half asleep and all. No thanks to you guys, though!"

I actually seemed to be doing quite well. Gerald thought I had sold more than any of them by the last part of August. As far as I knew, nobody had sold 71 Bibles in less than six weeks. I calculated that at this rate I would be selling nearly 560 Bibles in a year, netting about $4,000. I would be rich in just a few years. I was feeling on top of the world. I had found what I was really good at. Of course, that was before that last horrible sale that made all the difference and sent me hurrying back east to Rutgers University.

13

Episode 9: Shocking Success

By the third week in August we arrived in The Dalles, Oregon. Gerald dropped me off at a small, older hotel and I booked a room for a week. The Dalles was already large enough to keep us all busy that long. I have no idea where the others were housed. I had my section of the town to work in and I did not see them again until Friday.

The hotel was also called The Dalles. I found out it was owned and managed by a blind woman. She asked me about my schooling and urged me to go on with college. She felt one becomes a different kind of person if one makes the most of a college education.

She was a remarkable woman. I stopped in to say hello after every day out in the streets. We shared views of composers, poets and novelists. We also spoke a lot about the city of The Dalles and how she pictured its future. They were always very interesting conversations. I enjoyed them and I think she looked forward each day to my visit.

On Thursday I went directly to her door from a day of selling with no sales at all, and I was a little down, thinking a conversation with her would cheer me up.

Her companion, a very large and tough woman with a heart of gold and muscles of a wrestler, greeted me and escorted me into her sitting room. Gladys was all smiles and bubbling over with something.

"Guess what?" she challenged me.

"What?"

"I have received a letter!"

"I trust it was not an ordinary letter from the happy expression on your face!" I ventured.

"Not at all! Shall I read it to you?"

"I'm dying to hear it."

She read me the letter, not missing a single word. It was a very formal invitation to meet a man some distance away in Oregon. I didn't recognize the name, so I wasn't sure what to say.

"Who is he?" I finally ventured.

"You don't know?"

"I'm afraid not. Remember, I am not from these parts."

"Everybody knows about him. He is world famous and has traveled to almost every country in the world, lecturing and healing," she announced.

"Healing?" I asked. "You mean he is a doctor?"

"No, no. He is a genuine healer!"

"You mean a faith healer?"

"You make it sound a little cheap. He has done miracles. The newspapers have described some of the people who have gone to him and been miraculously healed. It got to the point he no longer saw people except by appointment. I wrote to him months ago and was beginning to despair I would ever hear from him. This is such good news! Congratulate me!"

"I do, I do." I probably was not enthusiastic enough, judging from the expression on her face.

"I'm sorry," I stammered. "I didn't know and I am not sure I completely understand. I am fond of you and it is a surprise to hear of this. Are you going there to be healed?"

"Yes."

"Has he restored anyone else's sight before?"

"Yes."

"How does he do it?"

"He doesn't do it at all. You have to understand that he does not do the healing. He is only a medium."

"Then how does it work? How are you healed?"

"It's my faith that does the healing. The strength of my faith in his presence brings healing forces to bear on me and my strong faith will give me my sight again."

"Is your faith that strong?" I wondered.

"More! Even more than you can imagine!"

Without thinking or making a decision, something instinctive in me pulled out the Bible I was selling and placed it in her lap.

"Is your faith so strong that you will buy something now that you can only use if your eyes can see again?"

Gladys was motionless. She felt the Bible and then bowed her head in silence. Her companion rose from her chair silently, moved stiffly to her purse on the table, and removed a $20 bill. She came to me and placed the bill in my hand. Without a word she opened the door to the apartment, inviting me to leave. I did.

I spent the entire Friday in a daze, going through the motions of calling on houses and extolling the virtues of this Bible. I had lost something. A spark had gone out of my selling and my will forces.

I barely made it through the day like an automaton, all the while feeling the blues settling around my shoulders.

I went right up to the door of Gladys' apartment and knocked. There was no answer. I knocked again, but still no answer. Then I understood. She no longer wanted to see me. I must admit I could not blame her.

14

COMMENTARY ON TURNING POINTS IN LIFE

July and August of that year were my very own two months. I had accepted the job of selling Bibles, not out of religious reasons or because I believed strongly in what I was doing. Looking back, I think I did it for a lark. It seemed exciting to arrive in a strange place, be all alone, and then meeting those interesting people that formed the sales team. I admired them for their free life and their personal choices. They were like a different species of birds, free to fly here and there wherever they liked. It suited my age to be like them and with them. I enjoyed moving freely from town to town.

My only compulsion was to sell enough so that I could cover my room and board as I traveled. I had only myself to look after. No classes to attend. No teachers to obey and imitate. I was 18 years old and on top of the world!

Every household I called on gave me examples of people caught or trapped in one kind of life or another. I was the free one; they were beneath me on the scale of independence. I relished the idea that I had mastered my existence and was being envied by my sales prospects, who often asked questions about my life style and seemed to display longings that I was fulfilling with my daily activity.

I was even proud of many of my sales conquests. We shared tales about triumphs each day. We vied with each other for the most incredible sale of the day. We laughed together about stories of the half-truths we told people in order to "make the sale." Nothing ever seemed evil or outright untruthful. It was just that, to be the best in this profession, one needed to wander a little from the straight and narrow because of the weakness in others. We had to play to their desires and illusions if we were going to eat and live.

Now something else had happened. The relationship with Gladys was different. Something of the nature of trust and honor had crept into the connection with this woman. That we shared elements of our lives in complete openness and honesty threw a different light on what we were to each other. It made us both vulnerable, which is what happens in a true human relationship. Shared vulnerability knits together deeper elements of the soul and demands a greater level of trust and responsibility. There was nothing about this in Mr. Barrett's training program. It was a major omission!

That's what I was feeling. I had betrayed something in another human being. I had taken advantage of her vulnerability and used it for my own benefit at her expense. I wondered what others would think of what I had done.

That evening we met in town and had a soup and sandwich supper before moving on to the next town. As usual we talked about the events of the week and I told my story. To my surprise Gerald, Lucy and Belinda laughed loudly, joshed me and congratulated me on an excellent sale. They even had suggestions on how I might have gotten more out of the situation, like selling a Bible to the companion as well. (Ha, ha!)

Thor did not say a word. He looked at me, a strange expression on his face, almost wonderingly, like, "Who are you?"

I took Gerald aside, returned to him two Bibles I had not sold, and informed him I was not going on with them.

"How come? You are doing so well!"

"I think I have found my senses. I am going back to Rutgers University where I had applied and been accepted. There is more to life than selling Bibles. I know now that I don't want to sell something; I want to contribute something. I want to know enough so that I can make a difference for good in the world," was my clumsy response.

"You are making a difference. Think of how many people may be reading the Bible again just because you gave them a chance to sacrifice some of their money to get it. A lot of people will be happier, more knowledgeable and stronger in their faith just because you entered their lives."

"It's hard to explain why I need something else."

"Try," he said.

"Do you know the Roman story of Mario?" I asked.

"No. Does it have something to do with your decision."

"Yes. I believe so."

"Tell it to me."

"There was a time, long ago, when the city of Rome suffered a tremendous earthquake. Houses tumbled and people and animals fell over each other in fear. An enormous crack appeared, running through the center of the forum, and a cavernous crevice divided the city.

"In those days when confronted with a problem people appealed to an Oracle for solutions. The way we consult scientists today, they consulted priests in a temple. When consulted the Oracle pronounced its solution. 'Rome must throw its most precious possessions into the crevice and it will close again.'

"Out of civic duty all the citizens of Rome began to throw their precious possessions into the great rift that separated them from each other. Jewels, silver and gold plates and ornaments were thrown in. Anything of value disappeared into the blackness and yet nothing happened. Romans began to despair. They thought maybe they would not have enough precious things to satisfy the Gods.

"Then Mario jumped on his horse and shouted loud for all to hear, 'Rome's most precious possessions are her sons!' He spurred his horse and rode into the crevice. Mario and horse disappeared and were never seen again, but the crevice closed with a powerful roar and the city was whole again.

"I have always admired that story and I admired Mario. Some people might think him foolish. I admired that he gave all he had for what he believed in. I know few of us get the chance to do it the way Mario did. I learned these last few months with you, Lucy, Belinda and Thor that most of us have to give our life in little bits and pieces every day. That's what we do, but it must be for something really important. Something we believe in.

"I know it is hard to explain, but that's what I am looking for; something worth giving my life for in bits and pieces every day."

Gerald looked at me curiously, then he shook my hand, wished me luck and we settled our accounts and parted.

I hitchhiked back across the country along the southern route and arrived at Rutgers University in time to register, select classes and begin my studies. I had survived two months without any guidance from home or from above, or so I thought at the time when my world was my oyster! I wonder what you think!

Was I being guided without noticing it? Was the invisible hand gesturing and pushing me as I strutted through the world, relishing every achievement. Even though I had graduated from High Mowing School and felt myself to be imbedded in the "real" world, was I actually still in school? Was I being taught and tested and challenged without knowing it?

❦

Who can say when school really ends and work starts?

Even though I had left High Mowing School behind, when the summer closed and I ventured back to New Brunswick, New Jersey, I felt somehow satisfied that the summer was all it was supposed to be. I was just a little bit wiser, calmer and more certain of who I was and what I was intended to do with the life I was given.

It was clear. This turning point took me back to continue where I left off before traveling west. It wasn't a detour, but it wasn't in a straight line either. Maybe in space it looked like a detour, but in time it appeared to be a continuation. Is it possible that those two months while thinking myself totally in charge of my own life actually were in my Angel's independent school? Was I being tutored one-on-one by my Angel as the last direct involvement of my youth? I began to see that recognizing my Angel meant staying continually awake to creative activity. The Angel's laws did not seem like strict rules to follow, but required unending creativity and flexibility. If we were working on a common biography together, were we also growing old together?

15

Fourth Conclusions about Angel Behavior

I think, however, that I discovered a bit more about how the angel works and interacts with me.

1. Learning may be one thing to professors and students. To them it is more like the acquisition of facts and opinions that slowly build up an abstract body that gradually solidifies and loses its flexibility. Such learning apparently does not impress the angel.
2. Angel learning seems more like growing. It is full of life and maturing. Perhaps as far as the angel is concerned there is just as much learning happening when there is no teaching or when no formal teaching is rolling itself out. Living is synonymous with learning. If we ever stop learning, we may be dying.
3. In two months I soaked up a lifetime of understanding and compassion for humanity. I saw it, lived with it, experienced it in myself and suffered with it at an age when everything sticks for a lifetime. I cannot recall a single person or experience that did not make an indelible impression. I can even go back in memory and find more learning and growth each time I revisit an episode or scene from those two months. If my Angel truly left me alone, was it because I was completely

alive to everything we both needed for our further development? I can even be grateful that an angel did not interfere in my life.

4. *Perhaps the angel, though more perfect than a human being, is still not perfect. Perfect may be another form of death and angels must live. Just as humans are at all stages of development, I now think angels are also at various stages of development.*

SECTION THREE

ANGEL ASSISTED EDUCATION

"Who can say when work begins? A lifetime includes 'work' transformed into soul work and at last spiritual work. It is we that become a church unto ourselves and there we find ourselves engaged with an angel."

16

Episode 10: A College Education with Pay

In those days Rutgers University was organized mostly for students from New Jersey. Since my parents lived in New Jersey, I qualified. Since Rutgers was a state university, the books I had to buy cost more than the tuition, especially since I qualified for a scholarship of $200. I don't believe I would have had an undergraduate degree if it had cost more.

The freshman year was tumultuous. The Korean War was over and veterans poured into universities with a maturity way above the average college student. Many were married with children. Many had experiences that left them impatient with most of the shenanigans of the freshman student group. All freshmen were forced to live in dorms, but there were not enough dorms. Most of us ended up at Fort Kilmer, an abandoned army recruitment base a few miles distant from the University. Buses carted us back and forth as needed.

By the end of the second semester, we all had to move out of the barracks and I decided I would rent a small apartment with a roommate. I also needed a job.

Right at the base of the main campus of Rutgers University was the George Washington Restaurant. I stopped in for coffee and there was Rose, the head waitress. Titles were not a big thing in restaurants, but she so obviously was in charge of the waitresses. She was working on the schedule.

"I am looking for a job."

"Are you a Rutgers student?"

"Yes, but I am a good worker and very reliable."

"I hope you can prove that to Jack," she said. "I only supervise the waitresses; I don't do the hiring."

"Who's Jack?"

"Mr. Troisi is the owner and boss."

"Where can I find him?"

"Probably in the basement."

"How do I get down there?"

She directed me through swinging doors, through the kitchen and down stairs in the back that led to the basement.

Jack was tall and very solid. He wore an apron over his white shirt and tie. He was checking boxes that had obviously just been delivered.

"Here, hold this," he ordered.

I wrapped my arms around a box and held it so he could check the label and numbers. It seemed to satisfy him and he pointed to a stack of other boxes for me to set it down.

"All these have to be put over there," he said. "Who are you?"

"Siegfried."

He looked at me unbelieving.

"It's true!" I assured him.

"Hey listen, it's OK. You can be whatever you like."

"But that's who I really am!"

He picked up one of the boxes, I picked up another and we started moving them into a far corner of the basement.

"Did you want something besides helping me, I mean?"

"Maybe helping you as much as I can and earning some pay along the way would be nice."

He grunted and buried his face in an order book, scribbling notes and adding up a column of figures. He chewed gently on the end of an unlit cigar, grunted again and stuck the pencil behind his ear.

"I never hired a Siegfried before!" He looked suspiciously at me. "Are you a student?"

"Rutgers," I said. "Start me now and you get at least three years out of me."

"I take it you want to start right away?"

"Yes."

"Well, you'll have to wait until 5:00."

"Great. I have a class that finishes at 4:50."

"You need to be here promptly at 5:00 to be any good to me. I can't have you dragging in anywhere from 5:00 to 5:30 every day."

"Every day?" I asked wonderingly.

"Yes. I expect you to be here every day from 12:00 to 2:00 and again from 5:00 to 8:00. Sometimes you'll have to be here from 5:00 to midnight to help close, especially when there has been a game."

"Thank you, I appreciate the chance to work for you." I paused, "What will I be doing?"

"Sometimes you'll be the busboy, maybe sometimes cleaning up the bathrooms. Other times you'll be operating the dishwasher, and other times you'll be helping me in the stock room. Is that OK with you?"

"Sure, as long as it isn't sitting around making conversation." I thought a little humor might be appropriate, but I felt great knowing I had a job.

And did I have a job! It was magnificent. For the next three years I spent 54 hours every week in the George Washington Restaurant. In between I went to classes. When I graduated I had a 3.2 average. Many years later, when a friend speculated on what my average would have been had I not worked so many hours of the week, I opined that it would have been lower. Those hours at the George Washington Restaurant saved me. If I had all that time in which to study, I doubt if I would have devoted myself to the books any more than I already did. I probably would have wasted my extra time and no doubt gotten into more trouble one way or another. I am grateful to Jack and the George Washington Restaurant for sparing me all that needless extra study. A higher grade would not have meant all that much in subsequent years anyway.

I was also grateful to all the employees in the George Washington Restaurant and even all the customers for giving me my real education, the one I was paid to receive while on the job. I learned more about life, about service, and about integrity at the George Washington Restaurant than I ever did at the University.

In the restaurant I learned about priorities. I discovered how the customers always had to be first, and if they were not, how to make them think they were first. There was no business without the customer. Suppose there was only one single customer all day. What did that mean? By rights that one customer should be charged the full overhead for a day. In other words, to be financially solvent Jack should be charging that one customer about $1,000 for his meal. The only way to avoid that was to have a second customer. The two of them could get their meals for $500 each. By the time we reached 100 customers a day, they would only have to pay $10 each for the same meal. I eventually found out we needed about 150 customers every day to break even and begin to make a profit. Every customer mattered, regardless what he or she looked like, how he or she dressed or how irritable he or she happened to be.

I also learned that customers had to like the food, but more than anything else, they had to feel important and that we, their servers, had to make them feel especially welcome and appreciated. A smile and a cheerful hello worked miracles. Humor worked wonders for some, while speed and efficiency impressed others. Some wanted to take their time and linger over a meal; others were always in a hurry. Some needed help in making a menu selection. Still others didn't like anything on the menu and needed to feel we were getting something off-menu especially for them.

I learned more about psychology at the George Washington Restaurant than in any of the advanced educational psychology classes at the University.

Then there were the other servers. One time I swept the tips off the table into a cup. The sound reverberated throughout the whole restaurant and servers came rushing over from all corners to protect their income.

"The busboy never touches the money," they explained emphatically. "The dishes, the glasses, the napkins, anything, but not the MONEY!"

Every penny was guarded jealously. Every tip meant more than money in their pockets and purses. It reassured them they were doing a good job. Once a customer left only what amounted to about 5% of the bill. The server looked at it, a shocked expression on her face, tears welled up in her eyes and she rushed after the customer and caught him at the exit door.

"Sir, what did I do wrong? I tried to serve you in the best possible way! What did I do?"

"Why, nothing. You were excellent and the food was delicious!"

"Then why the small gratuity?"

"Small gratuity?" he asked puzzled. "Let me see that." He reached for the copy of the bill he had in his pocket.

"Oh, my God! I made a mistake. I guess I was talking too much and didn't figure it right. Sorry!"

He handed the server a $20 bill, apologizing profusely and left. Through her tears the server was mollified and returned to her work.

The tips communicated more loudly than any words. Compliments were always welcome and usually deserved, but the real complimentary shouting was done through the size of the tip. Every server worth anything learned to behave in a way that would result in a favorable tip.

I also learned that there is always something to do when you are working in a restaurant. Once all customers had been served, or in the lulls between rush times, there was time to catch up on cleanups, find fresh sponges and rags, restock the shelves and the ice cream containers, refill the syrup pumps, and make fresh coffee. The coffee ran out so quickly, it always had to be made fresh.

Jack was an incredible boss. With a certain brash humor and make-believe toughness, he kept the whole place humming like a happy beehive. He taught us to be respectful of each other and of the customers. He taught us to make every customer feel good about the food and the service. From him, either directly or through just being in his restaurant, I learned the essences of good business practice.

Episode 10: A College Education with Pay

Actually the combination of Rutgers University classes and work at the George Washington Restaurant was unbeatable. At Rutgers I learned about theoretical psychology, literature, biology and grades.

When Dr. Kirk gave me a failing mark, it really hurt. I had filled three essay books, working furiously the whole hour with all I knew about Chaucer. He corrected some spelling mistakes and a bit of grammar here and there and marked it an F. No comment about some of my insights or comparisons with other authors and storytellers. I was exacerbated and determined to prove him in error.

When I arrived at his office, he was on the phone. He waved me into a chair and went on with his phone conversation. The office was very small, much too small for the piles of books covering every available level space. The three bookshelves that lined the walls were also jammed with books. I glanced at some of the titles; all books about the Middle Ages and poets and authors from that time. There was no doubt that this was the office of a scholar and leading authority on the age of Chaucer.

Dr. Kirk sat behind his desk, the phone buried in his snow-white hair. His dry voice crackled authoritatively into the phone, disagreeing about the source of a reference I had never heard of. Behind him, hanging on the wall beside the only window in the office, was a black relief presentation of a profile imbedded in an ivory background. The profile looked familiar, but I couldn't quite place it and I frowned trying to stimulate a recollection from High Mowing School. Finally I remembered just as Dr. Kirk hung up the phone and turned to face me.

"So, you don't think a failing grade is fair! Is that right?"

"No sir," I insisted. "It does not accurately reflect what I really learned and know about Chaucer, thanks in large part to you, Sir!"

He reached for my test books, bunched together in a folder. He began looking through them, smirking, I thought, at what I had written. I thought maybe it would help if I could change the focus from my test books to something more complementary to him.

"I was admiring your relief of the head of Savonarola. It seems an exceptionally finely carved piece. Although Savonarola seems odd given your thorough devotion to Chaucer." I smiled at him, thinking I was sliding in a complement.

"Savonarola, you say? That, my dear fellow, happens to be Chaucer. Do you still wonder why you received a failing grade?"

"That couldn't possibly be Chaucer, even though the features are somewhat similar!" I maintained with absolute certainty, thinking back on the days at High Mowing School in the living room in Mrs. Emmet's house. She had summed up Chaucer in the most vibrant tones. I could visualize him, his features wrinkled in laughter, then smiling, then exuding empathy for all of our foibles and idiosyncrasies. I could never forget the varying expressions on that imaginary face of Chaucer.

"But it is Chaucer! Do you think I would want the bust of Savonarola hanging over me all these years?" he exploded indignantly.

"If that relief was done by an artist, which it probably was, judging by the fine craftsmanship, then it could not be Chaucer!"

"What is your reason, may I ask?" Sarcasm dripped from his curled lip.

"To do Chaucer in stark black and white would be an insult, not a tribute. Any artist doing Chaucer would insist on some color. The idea of doing him in black and white would make an artist shudder! Every one of his characters in the Canterbury Tales is colorful to say the least! His mind as a writer took in color automatically. He saw his characters in color judging by his descriptions."

Dr. Kirk was silent. He pursed his lips and brought his pencil to them thoughtfully. I took courage from this and went on.

"On the other hand, any artist doing Savonarola would automatically want to do it in black and white. With Savonarola everything was either black or white, either good or evil. There were even no shades of grey. The idea of color, a whole spectrum between black and white, wouldn't interest him at all. He ignored any exception. If someone was not good, then he had to be bad. That was his character and black and white were his medium. The whole of medieval England bowed to his distorted image of reality."

"Well, you make an interesting case. Too bad I know for a fact that this piece of art was definitely intended to represent Chaucer and that's why a friend purchased it and gave it to me."

It was my turn to be silent.

"I am sorry to have to give you this failing grade, but your grammar and spelling were atrocious and every one of your ideas were not distilled from scholarship, but from conjecture and personal feelings. If we are going to make any kinds of statements, we need to make sure they are true and not simply preferred prejudices. That's why scholarship exists, so that we can restrict our knowledge and our opinions to what is true. No, no, I am sorry!" he added as I found an opening in his remarks and was about to argue.

I left his office as the phone rang again and he lifted the receiver, waving me out with his left hand.

A week later I received a short note. Scribbled on his personal stationary were the terse words, "It is Savonarola. Revised Grade is C+."

Some people think this is a nice little story, but it shows nothing of a supernatural presence. In other words, there are no footprints of an angel to be seen. They would be right, because often it takes a high degree of sensibility to discern an angel's footprint. First of all one has to acknowledge the presence of a footprint, namely that a form in time reveals something of the passing of a living creature. If you are one of those people who do not see soul prints in biographical material, then you must exert yourself to enhance your perceptions.

You are like someone who observes a hole in the ground and cannot distinguish between a wormhole, one that is made by the beak of a bird, another that is made by a fallen branch, and still another that is made by the passing of a deer. Each has its own character made by a cause, but to you they are just holes in the ground having different shapes. As to causes, they do not reveal anything useful to you. After all, they are just holes in the ground.

The same is true of our human inner life. No doubt you think our thoughts and feelings are random and reveal nothing except interesting connections to the past or genetic construction. The fact that they and not some others arise is simply accidental in nature for you. They just happen to surface in the mind. Sometimes we make use of them and other times we do not.

In the course of a lifetime, thousands of useful ideas, and feelings surface with meaningful utility and artistically shape the contours of a personal biography, defying analytical chance and seeming to carry little weight for psychologists or philosophers. We don't even see most of the angel's footprints, because we don't look for them. It is easy to deny what we deliberately choose not to see.

The fact is simply this. We attribute all the mysterious wisdom-filled events and choices in our life either to our own cleverness, or if we cannot fairly do so, to something we call chance, which is just another way of saying, "I don't know!" It is surprising how many of us feel absolutely content with "I don't know" as a conclusion without looking a little further and going beyond our immediate sense impressions. We are materialists absolutely stuck deep in the mirage of our own sense impressions.

Two years before this event in college, I was called into Mrs. Emmet's presence at High Mowing School to defend a comment I had made about the difficulty of reading Chaucer and his endless detailed descriptions.

"If you had to decide something, anything about Chaucer's character, what would it be?" she demanded to know.

"I don't know, but he sure spent a lot of time on describing gobs of details that seem to me to have very little to do with any action or plot. Give me a story and a plot any day!" I insisted.

"Is that all you can say about Chaucer?"

"Well, I think he loved his characters to spend so much time describing them. I think he also relished sounds and colors, oh, and differences between people. Not two are the same. Each is unique. He is also pretty daring to write some of the things he described his characters doing. I doubt if any of my teachers here would be happy if I described what he did, I mean some of it, anyway."

"You mentioned color?" She prompted me.

"Well, I mean he distinguished nuances of color, some of the names of colors we don't use very much any more today. And he reveled in them, I mean he seemed to enjoy them. I bet he had very good eyes. Also he must have loved colors almost as much as he loved peculiarities in character and sensibilities. Actually, he must have been a good writer!" I admitted this.

Mrs. Emmet smiled and dismissed me. "Don't you have any homework you should be doing right now, Dearie?" she asked. I left, feeling that maybe she liked me after all, for all the trouble I was always causing her.

It was one of the few times she worked me over in person. Is that why I remembered the interview so well? Every expression on her wrinkled face, the way she pursed her lips and brought the eraser end of the pencil to them, even the wreath of delicate, light grey hair giving her a modest halo. I remember every word.

How interesting that of all the four years of experiences at High Mowing School in Wilton, New Hampshire, this one episode should provide me with such good use. At the time it rang with a kind of inner tone or light, as though saying to me in the only way it could, "Take note, remember, hold on to this, it has meaning for your life!"

Who was it that was so tenderly touching me? What was it that played around the edges of my consciousness? What made me so especially awake at an age I generally slept with wide-open eyes? Is it again you, my co-creator of this biography? Were you again near, touching both of us with attentiveness because something meaningful was taking place?

I also learned that I do not always have to wait until my Angel has already passed me by and left a footprint for me to recollect. I learned that if I am sensitive enough I can begin to discern how near or how far my Angel is. When she approached and only when she was near, there was a feeling of a kind of humming or tone or light sensation, not in my eyes or ears, but in my soul. It is almost as if my soul begins to vibrate when my Angel draws near.

It was a new way of being for me. I now walked about in life with a heart open to the possibility that every now and then I would feel her presence. It was never dominant, only suggestive, simply another aspect of experience to take into account as I made decisions or acted. Although I was always responsible for what I thought, or did, from then on I always opened myself to her influence.

Sometimes, out of nowhere, even while doing something insignificant, the telltale sensations would become noticeable. On every such occasion I would feel the delicate vibrations, a fine tonal sensation, warning me, alerting me to a presence, warming me to openness. I learned to pay attention and watch for "sign" the way a tracker looks for sign. The Angel whose biography is intertwined with mine was making her presence felt.

17

Episode 11: Sex Education

One of the most faithful customers at the George Washington Restaurant always sat at the end of the counter. Everyone called her Honey and so did I. She had a secretive smile not unlike the Mona Lisa and often regarded me from half-closed eyes while she ate. I chatted with her as did everyone else as they passed the end of the counter on their way to the kitchen or to the tables.

My brother lived in Clinton, New Jersey, a twenty-minute drive from Rutgers University. When he called I was surprised; he usually dropped in on his way to somewhere else.

"How about we take in a movie tonight?" he offered.

"Sure, I get off at 8:00. You want to pick me up?"

"Yeah. I have a date with me. You want me to bring a blind date for you?"

I looked over at Honey. She smiled.

"No, I think I can find somebody to bring along."

It was a pleasant evening. I really did watch the movie. Honey held on to my hand throughout the entire movie, except when I put my arm around her when she nestled against my shoulder, seemingly quite content.

After the movie my brother drove us to Honey's house and she and I got out. My brother asked whether he should pick me up. I said no, I'll find my way home.

"Don't turn on the lights," Honey demanded as we entered through the door.

"Why not?"

"I like it this way!" she said.

I took her in my arms and began my elaborate seduction process. I say elaborate because I didn't know what I was doing. Every time I started to work on a button or zipper, she took my hand away and put it somewhere else.

This continued for nearly two hours. I was rapidly tiring but Honey seemed never to have enough of my company. We were first on a couch, then against one of the walls and finally on the floor. Still, I was confused. Did she want me to make love to her or didn't she? Was I doing something wrong? Then I became suspicious.

"Are we alone here?" I asked

"Of course, silly!" she gurgled into my ear.

"Then why can't we turn on the lights?"

"Don't you think this is nice?"

"Sure, but I have a funny feeling something isn't quite right. Are you afraid someone might see us?"

"Oh no! I just like being in the dark like this."

"Well, I am certainly in the dark. Hopelessly in the dark! Maybe I should call a cab and make my way home," I finally suggested.

"Oh no, this is so nice and peaceful. You are such a nice guy! Stay a little longer!"

I returned to my arduous exercise and made no more headway than before. Finally I looked at my watch.

"My goodness, it's already 2:00 a.m. I really must be going."

She clung to me as I made my way to the door. I persuaded her to phone for a taxi, in the dark no less, and left.

"You just don't understand women," my brother explained. He was eight years older than I, so he had the right to enlighten me. "Women don't want what men want. What I mean is that each woman is a universe to herself. Without the right key, you are banging your head against the door. Always—and I really mean *always*—look for the key. You know what I mean?"

"Well, I suppose...," I ventured, before he cut me off.

"Let me tell you what happened to me the first time. You know I was working on a farm in Pennsylvania. All the summer help lived in a kind of farm-run rooming barracks. This one girl was really saucy. She flirted with everyone, and we had a lot of good laughs. One day, she suggested I come to her room after all the lights were out and the whole house was quiet.

"At her room, I knocked softly so as not to create a disturbance. I had especially showered and shaved and wore a clean shirt and overalls.

"'Come in,' she whispered, loud enough for me to hear through the door.

"I entered. The room was dark, and it took a while before shapes of furniture and walls became visible. She was lying on her bed. I touched her in the dark, groping my way to the bed. She was naked.

"I couldn't believe my good luck. This was better than anything I could have dreamed of. With a single motion I stripped off my clothes and jumped on top of her, joyously and ready. She screamed at the top of her voice, punched, pushed and kicked me off the bed and out of the room. What did I do wrong? Wasn't I just doing what she wanted me to do? In a daze I ran down the hall, trailing my clothes, past the open doorways of all the other rooms, past a variety of other comments and sleepy questions and slipped into my own room.

"That was my first experience with women, and also how I lost a very good white shirt."

"I don't think I would have done that!" I protested.

"All I'm saying is that until you find the right key every woman is a closed, locked world within herself. It's you searching for the key that she loves most. Learn to enjoy the searching!"

18

Episode 12: Romance

Although I had a very special friend and love during high school at High Mowing that I never quite managed to forget, it wasn't until Sally and her friend Sarah ordered soda at the counter that I met again someone special. The two of them were accompanied by Sarah's boyfriend Warren, who was a chubby, lovable guy with never an unkind or critical word to say. He was a delightful companion and engaged me in conversation while Sally challenged me with her eyes. I don't remember exactly how it happened, but all of a sudden I seemed to be "going" with her. She was only sixteen years old while I had reached the exalted stage of 20.

Sally was a treasure. She was lively, lovely in appearance, often bitingly funny as she commented on what she experienced in people and the world. Her intellect had been sharpened along the way and while I was in her company I never had to worry about something to say. She took care of all our agendas and managed our conversations ably.

"Let's go for a drive," she suggested one time.

"I don't have a car, as you well know, Sally."

"My parents want to meet you anyway. Can you come over to my home before we go out?"

"OK, but we'll have to take the bus to wherever we are going."

When I arrived at their apartment near the University, I was met at the door by the two nicest people you could ever find. They were so open and hospitable. In no time they both had me talking about my studies, my job at the restaurant, my hopes for the future. Sally's parents were an absolute joy to meet and know.

"Dad says we can use the car," Sally announced.

"You do have a license, I presume," he called out as I helped Sally into her coat.

"Yes."

"Good, our car works better that way."

"Do be careful," her mother urged at the door. "The Merc is the only car we have, and Dad needs it to get to work."

"Well, if worse came to worse I could get one of the trucks," Dad volunteered from the other room.

They hardly knew me, but they trusted me. They trusted me with their car and also with their daughter. She was only sixteen and I was twenty and still they trusted me. They had both gone to college and surely remembered what it was like to be twenty, and still to trust me just floored me.

We were together until my graduation. One time we had been smooching fairly seriously. Somehow her clothes began to disappear and some of mine also vanished. I suddenly saw in her eyes and felt it in the temperature of the room that I had found the key, whatever that was. I found it and couldn't use it. Somehow I was restrained by the powerful trust with which her parents had bound me. For all my affection for her, all the wonderful times we experienced together, all the energy of our youth, I could not betray those trusting eyes of her father and mother.

One of my friends from High Mowing School told me he was looking for an apartment in New York City. How about we rent it together? He knew I wanted to write and thought being in the City would give me a chance to write and be decadent. I jumped at this opportunity. It had always been a dream to write stories and novels and even poetry.

"Sally, I am sorry. I am twenty years old and I need this chance to devote myself entirely to writing."

"You can still do that and go on seeing me. I would not interfere at all. Maybe now and then you feel like driving out here again and we could see each other. I might be able to take the train into New York and see you that way. If we want to see each other and be together, I am sure we'll manage it somehow."

"I need to be totally free. I don't want any obligations or responsibilities. I don't know of any wild oats, but if there are any I want to sow them now."

"You can sow them with me."

"No Sally, sorry. Please understand my predicament. I am terribly fond of you and hurting you is the last thing I would ever want to do, but if I don't take this chance to be absolutely clear and free of any attachments, I will never find this chance again. I am sure of that."

"You don't love me."

"I do. Maybe I am making a big mistake and maybe I'll come crawling back, but I need this chance to write and be dissolute."

"We never even made love!" Tears welled up in her eyes.

"Perhaps it is for the best."

"I don't even have that!"

"Sally, you are the most wonderful person I could have been with these past two years. Know that I will always treasure our time together."

"You are dumping me, that's what I know."

"No, I am carving out a private space for myself and I don't know what will become of it!"

"One does not throw precious things away. You will regret what you are doing!"

With that she left me. I have not seen her since. That was 55 years ago. I still have not written the novel that lived in my mind and replaced her in my heart. However, the slate was clear and I found myself free to shape and live my biography.

Little did I know that I would be a husband within ten months and a father within another ten months. If you had told me that would happen, I would not have believed you. I would have accused you of insanity.

19

Episode 13: Love

My mother told me, "There is a study group meeting in New York City. They study Rudolf Steiner. I think you should go."

"You know, I am very busy. I work long hours at the newspaper, and I am also trying to write some short stories. I don't have time for sitting around arguing philosophy."

"It's every Wednesday evening at 7:30 at 15 East 56th Street. They study *The Philosophy of Freedom* by Rudolf Steiner."

"Thanks for letting me know!" I ended the conversation.

"I think you should go!" She looked at me, a peculiar expression on her face. "It's for young people."

"I'll talk to you later." I was not intending to go and promptly forgot about it.

On Wednesday afternoon, the *Daily News* let me know I was not needed on the night shift. Don't ask me why. I had just finished the short story I was writing. It was too long, and I knew it had to be cut drastically. Cutting required a different mind-set, and I was not up to it. Unexpectedly, I had a whole evening to myself, the first in a long time and I was lost. What to do?

I left the apartment and started walking down Broadway. I stopped now and then to watch interesting antics of people, a favorite hobby of mine and very helpful for writing stories. I passed Columbus circle, looked around for a coffee shop and saw

Horn and Hardart, an automat offering inexpensive sandwiches and other food. I was well into my sandwich before it dawned on me where I was.

It was Wednesday evening, pretty close to 7:30 and on 56th Street. I was not one to shirk away from so many omens. I looked for the address, rang the bell, climbed a flight of steps and entered a room full of younger people, all talking very earnestly with each other. Ruth Alexander greeted me, welcomed me, and I knew at once I was there for a good reason. She was incredibly beautiful, with a wide flawless smile, intelligent, awake eyes and a personal style that signaled a cultured upbringing and deeply cultivated manners. She was a lady without a doubt. I tingled with I knew not what and felt the familiar humming inside. She introduced me to the others, called the meeting to order and started the discussion with a question.

I remember very little of the evening's discussion, but I remember every gesture Ruth made and every facial expression became memorable.

"Well," she said at the door. "How did you like it?"

"I don't know," I ventured. "It's a little too much like a bull session at college, which I usually avoided."

"We're pretty open here. Why don't you help make it better?"

"I'll think about it."

"See you next week." She smiled

I had already studied a book by Rudolf Steiner, ominously titled *Occult Science*. I had studied it the way one does a text at college. I scribbled all over the pages, charted some of the more complex descriptions to get it right, and then left it alone for another think.

The very next day I went to a bookstore at 211 Madison Avenue and bought *The Philosophy of Freedom* by Rudolf Steiner. At home

I got to work poring over every sentence and struggling to understand the difficult passages. My head ached with the strain.

This was not something to swallow easily. Every sentence challenged me to think. I argued with Steiner on every page, not because I disagreed or found it strange, but because he challenged every easy conclusion of my life and demanded more of me than any other teacher or writer. Strangely enough, every one of his thoughts sounded familiar, as if I had heard them before or thought them at another time and place.

I drew charts and lists, juxtaposing various conclusions opposite each other on the paper, rearranging the words and thoughts in my own words.

The following Wednesday I was thoroughly prepared, as were several others in the group, and we went at it with a vengeance. At one point we were all on the floor leaning over different charts, making statements, correcting with each other and arriving at various agreements and ways of rephrasing.

That was the beginning of a study that lasted three years. Finally on the third go-round with the same book, many of us had broken through to a lifetime understanding of body, soul, spirit, karma, destiny, freedom, time and space. Not that we didn't continue to develop understanding and nurture the relationship of ideas to life, but somehow, as a result of such a deep study, we had a tentative foundation on which to build our biographies more consciously.

20

Episode 14: The Annunciation

By late Spring my stressful life style, working at the newspaper at night, writing by day and wasting considerable time posing as an artist in Greenwich Village, happily soaking up the decadent, creative atmosphere in the coffee shops, began to show in my pale face. I read some poetry at a late nightclub, argued the meaning of life and felt like I was really in the thick of important events.

"You look a little pasty," Ruth commented as we drank coffee after one of our meetings.

"I've been working and living too much."

"The wrong kind of living is my guess. You need some time in the country, away from the city, enjoying the healing influences of nature."

"I guess maybe I do."

"Denny and I are going to be camp counselors at Camp Glen Brook this summer in Marlborough, New Hampshire. Why don't you come with us?" Ruth asked.

"What would I do?"

"I don't know. Let's talk to Mr. Harrer and DJ, who own the camp. They are teachers at the Rudolf Steiner School here in the city. Since you went to that school and they probably know you, they might give you a summer job."

"It would be nice to be together, the three of us, in camp."

"Yes!" she agreed. "Three good friends!"

"How do you know I'm not in love with you?"

"How could you be? You've never said a word!"

"Well, I'm only asking. How do we know?"

Ruth looked at me, said not a word and let it pass.

By the middle of June we were all three in Marlborough, New Hampshire, getting the camp ready for opening day. It was a lot of cleaning and repairing, painting and disinfecting, but the weather was grand and the altitude and the view of Mt. Monadnock was refreshing and healing. William Harrer and his wife Dorothy Harrer, known as DJ, called meetings with us and a few other counselors as they began arriving to work on schedules and responsibilities.

"For parents' weekend, after the first four weeks, we like to put on a performance of something to show the parents," DJ said somewhat wistfully, looking around as if for inspiration or a response.

"Like what?" I asked.

"I don't know, but in past years we recited poetry, sang songs or played instruments. Maybe a recorder concert would work? In the first week we take all the campers over to Ocean Born Mary's house in Henniker. Maybe we could do something to tie in with that well-known Legend of Captain Pedro. Have you seen the little brochure they give to all the visitors?"

DJ handed the folder around for us to see. I read the story of Captain Pedro.

"This is great." I was enchanted by the story. "Maybe we should write a little play around the story."

"It could have songs in it, and some humor, and it could be performed on the front porch of the main building," Denny suggested. She was very artistic and a talented musician.

In no time at all, three or four of us suggested various approaches. I said I would be happy to write the script, and if others could deal with the songs and music under Denny's direction, we could have it ready by parents' weekend."

Denny worked on the opening songs and some of the choruses. Ruth came up with one of the songs. The script determined the songs because usually a scene change or mood change required an interlude.

I wrote one monologue and then just had to put sound to it, seeing how it meant so much to me.

"When I was a boy
And the world was new
My mother made a doll like this for me.
I lost it long ago at sea
But sometimes in the night
I see my mother's eyes
And hear her voice
Against my ears
Now that I am a man
And the world is no longer new."

I sang it for Denny and with her remarkable skill she captured it, melody and accompaniment. It became Captain Pedro's signature song for the little musical.

By the time some 50-plus children in ages from 7 to 11 arrived, we were still writing and composing, but rehearsals could begin. Denny began singing the songs with the children during her classes and pretty soon they were singing some of the more lively tunes on their way from the dining room to the barn, to the lake and on many a hike. They knew the songs by heart long before parents' day approached. Rehearsals began in earnest, different scenes with different children, but it all came together for dress rehearsal and the performance. "Ocean Born Mary" was a hit.

Denny, Ruth and I were friends for life.

"I think you three are born to teach in the Waldorf school. There the teaching is enlivened through music, song, art, games and circle activity, and you three seem destined to integrate everything you know how to do with what children need to know. What do you say?"

Mr. Harrer looked at his wife, a shocked expression and some warning glances shot at her. I found out later that he was the treasurer of the Rudolf Steiner School and still trying to balance the next year's budget.

"That's what I want to do. I am ready!" Denny was the first to respond.

"I love children and I would so much enjoy teaching in a Waldorf school." Ruth was certain of that.

"I don't know. I had dreamed of being a writer, but it hasn't yet fallen in place. In other words, I have not sold a single story or earned a dime, except on salary at the Daily News on which I turned my back in June," was all I could say.

DJ squinted at me through her glasses, a slight smile on her face that betrayed her complete confidence in life and what it had to offer.

Ruth had five girls in her room at the main house. I had six little boys in my room at the hill house. Everyday after lunch a rest period was scheduled. None of the children wanted to sleep.

"You do not have to sleep," we counselors explained. "All you do is take out one of your books or letters from home and read for a short time. This is a rest time, a quiet time, a time to recharge strength for the activities of the afternoon. There is no talking; you rest on your bed, and there is absolute quiet."

Fifteen minutes later they would all be asleep, including the counselors. There was so much wisdom in the schedule.

I had one day a week off from after rest period until midnight. Ruth and I ended up together on our days off. Mr. Harrer loaned us one of the station wagons of the camp. We went sightseeing and sometimes took in a movie in Keene. It was amazing how quiet the world seemed without fifty children and their overpowering energy.

One time after a movie we drove back to the camp, parked down by the lake and admired the moonlit night. In those days we could hear the crickets and tree frogs. The night was peacefully alive with a great concert of small sounds.

I leaned my head back against the headrest, closed my eyes and let the different instruments of the night surround me and relax my soul. A great peace descended over me. It was such a long time since I had such a deep feeling of peace. As if by the force of habit, I sank slowly into a welcoming void. I emptied myself of all thoughts. It was not hard to do. It came so naturally.

There I was in the car, my head leaned back against the headrest, Ruth beside me in the car. Her eyes were closed. The night enveloped the whole picture with its mystery. I gazed at it as if from above with my eyes closed, wrapped in the deep emptiness of feeling and sensation. Gradually a sensation rose in me, a definite feeling. I was being signaled by something present in my lower consciousness, at least it seemed lower but without specific direction of entry. I felt a kind of formative force. An artist was at work on my consciousness and soft mist, color sensations eddied at the fringes of my consciousness.

It formed and then dissolved again and then formed more clearly. A face looked at me with the friendliest expression. It was very round, blond, still childishly unformed. It was a child. It's expression sharpened and it looked right at me, almost accusingly, demanding something of me. Then a blinding realization! It shocked me right to the core.

"You are my son!" I thought. I might have whispered it, but I thought it so loud I am sure I could have said it. In that moment I was so overcome with the insight that I fell helter skelter out of the void and turned to Ruth to tell her what I had just experienced. I wanted to tell her I had just seen my future child, a son that would be important; a son that was determined to have a life.

As I turned to Ruth, looking at her directly, to describe what I had seen, another blinding insight. What a silly way to put it. An insight cannot be blinding. Insight must be brilliant, but not blinding. It felt blinding because it was so bright it took my breath away. Here, sitting in the front seat of the car, was the mother of that son. There was nothing vague about it; no doubt had a chance! This was the mother of the son I had just witnessed in the void.

"Will you marry me?" was how it came out. "I want you to marry me!"

"Why?" Ruth stammered, taken aback with the suddenness and forcefulness of my request.

"Because I love you and for the sake of my son who needs us both."

I then described to her what I had experienced. She took it all in quite naturally as if she knew, the way mothers almost always seem to know in some special way. I am not sure now whether Ruth ever actually accepted my proposal, or whether I just took it for granted. How else could she respond with so many incredible omens encouraging us?

21

Episode 15: The Rainbow

Three weeks later on a Sunday evening we were married. By chance we found a lovely chapel on a lake that was part of an estate that granted us permission to use it for a wedding. Denny was maid of honor. Paul Rettig, one of the counselors and a good friend, was best man. We did not have the time nor the money to shop for a ring, but we found curtain rings that fit loosely for the occasion. (The "ring that binds" seems to have worked, judging by the 60 years that followed!)

It was raining that day. Ruth and I, who were understandably sensitive to omens, wondered whether we were doing the right thing. It poured all night and hovered over us in the early dawn, then poured again. During the ceremony, just as the Minister asked for the ring and while I placed it on Ruth's finger, a triple rainbow spread its spectrum in concentric half circles across the sky over the lake beside the chapel. It sprang from the pines at the edge of the lake, crowned the heights and touched the greenery in the north. At last we had enough of an omen to assure us we were doing the right thing. Was this not a sure sign our marriage was fully sanctioned by the ruling hierarchies?

During the next 60 years we learned a great deal about marriage. It turned out to be something alive, invisible and incredibly deep.

Marriage is not an object, like a vase or a lawnmower. True, there is a piece of paper called a Marriage License that can be used to prove a marriage is being attempted. The piece of paper is not the marriage. In some miraculous way two people find each other. There are many millions of potential partners spread over the entire earth globe. Each potential partner represents a different culture, education, upbringing, and hereditary sources. This does not include differences in personality, tastes, preferences, ambitions, etc. The differences between individuals seems far greater than the differences in race, religion, and even greater than the differences between male and female. In looking for a partner the criteria to use is immense.

Even though the opportunities for travel and communication are far advanced in our time, that two people should find each other among the throngs is truly miraculous. Even selecting the best fit doesn't work, as the underlying assumption is that each of us knows what is best for us.

It seems that most of us take a lifetime to learn whether we are connected in marriage to the right person. How many people are potentially the right one for each of us? Looking for the "right one" begins to look hopeless. Unless, you are willing to factor in "accident." In reality, most of us discover our partners by curious routes and by curious circumstances. Very few of us can say, "I knew exactly what I wanted in a partner, knew where to look, and I systematically went looking for that person." Most of us have to admit something like, "I didn't want or mean to go there, and it wasn't at all what I expected, but there that one was."

You may believe what you like, but my life has enough evidence in it to factor in the "behind the scenes" wisdom filled choreography of my Angel. I cannot explain in any other way the vast blessing of the "right marriage."

Regardless of the mistaken conclusions of scientists that marriage is a natural phenomenon, my evidence shows me that it has almost nothing to do with the natural order. Marriage is almost in spite of the natural order.

Why should anyone risk their well-being, their personal freedom and carefree state in order to vow allegiance for a lifetime to another person. There is nothing in the marriage state that one could not obtain without it. It is a purely human creation in time. It cannot be done alone, it always requires another, it only lives as long as it is wanted, and it usually decays unless every day and night it is recreated. It is the most unusual creation of humans, as it only exists in a state of free will. Forced marriages, whether by our own will or by someone else, cannot remain alive. It may endure as a kind of life sentence, but it cannot be alive unless both parties found it through free will.

Are marriages made in heaven? The saying can be useful to us. We know there are all kinds of marriages. Actually, no two are the same. Each one is unique. Each marriage is only what those two particular individuals are able to create.

What interests me is the decision itself, the decision to commit for better or for worse to another person. How are we able to do that? Of course there is love and certainly it constitutes the bedrock of any marriage, but there must be more or the vow would not include "for better or worse." We normally avoid anything that is "worse." It is not our habit to seek out or continue to endure pain or suffering. Why should it matter that we vow to continue in a supportive relationship, even through "worse?"

As a matter of fact, why should our angel stick with us for a whole life for better or worse? Is the act of commitment modeled for us by our individual angel? Think what a song and dance we lead our angel through in every lifetime! Think what kind of commitment is required by our angel to stick with us through the whole of our biography.

A marriage is only the first step in our further development as humans. If we are unable to commit (in any way we choose) to one other person, then we no longer follow the example of our angel.

How can we carry ideals about caring for humanity and caring for the earth if we can't really commit to one person? The starting point to a better future is right here.

22

Commentary about How Angels Collaborate

Ruth was born in Berlin. She and her mother then lived in Switzerland, but ended up in Danzig, Germany, for her teen years. Her father was a British diplomat and ended up after World War II in the part of Germany controlled by the British. He sat at dinner one evening next to someone who recognized his name and knew Ruth and her mother.

He got them both out of the Russian Sector. To find out how he did it you will have to ask her about the dramatic escape.

When her father was asked to move to New York to represent the UK in the Economic and Social Council of the United Nations, Ruth jumped at the chance to come with him and his family. They lived in Garden City, Long Island, where there just happened to be a Waldorf School affiliated with Adelphi University. Ruth attended the University for two years and then transferred to Swarthmore College in Swarthmore, Pennsylvania. After graduation she took an apartment in New York City with a roommate. The roommate was Denny Rettig who was hoping to teach at the Rudolf Steiner School in New York City.

I met them both in the study group on the work of Rudolf Steiner that Ruth started.

I was also born in Germany, in Heilbronn, to be exact. My mother divorced my biological father and brought my brother and me to the United States in 1935, just before the war. I celebrated my third birthday on Ellis Island on April 2, 1935. I attended the Rudolf Steiner School in New York City until the 6th grade.

Grades 6 to 8 were in Orange, New Jersey. My mother had remarried Hans Just shortly after they purchased the small apartment house on Central Park West. When he took the job at Edison Company in Orange, New Jersey, my relationship with Hans Just—and, to be fair, also my mother—became increasingly difficult as I blundered into my teens.

"This is the third time you have run away and we have had to find you and bring you back," my stepfather accused me. "I have the impression you do not want to be here with your mother and I. So, I have come to a conclusion. Rather than have you run away and cause us all kinds of worry, I would prefer to send you away. Mrs. Emmet, the head of High Mowing School, has agreed to take you on trial for a semester. We cannot pay very much for your tuition, room and board, so I promised you would be a good student and help out in the kitchen, doing dishes, pots and whatever else you are asked to do."

"Sure," I agreed, already excited by the prospect of being somewhere else. My mother cried a little, and I agreed to send my laundry home every few weeks for her to wash and return to me. There were always a few cookies in the box.

Four years at High Mowing School were the most wonderful years for me. The dorm counselors were great, the teachers were magnificent, and my fellow students were all creative and unique personalities. I treasure every memory from those few years.

I graduated and subsequently enrolled at Rutgers University in New Bruswick, New Jersey. The moment I had my BA, I left friends and even a sweetheart to lodge myself in New York City. I was driven to be there for what reason I did not know. The picture in my mind was to be a writer of fiction, and what better place to try that than a big exciting city full of temptations.

Then came the study group where Ruth and I finally met.

Now I ask you, just look at those two stories, the one Ruth lived and the one I lived. Jump around from Germany to Switzerland to England and then New Jersey and New York where we two finally caught up with each other in a study group of all places. Our marriage was a sixty-year adventure resulting in three children, two foster children and at this writing seven grandchildren.

If I were really very smart and knew ahead of time that Ruth was just the right person for me and that we could so marvelously navigate those years together, could I have engineered the intricate arrangements and events to bring us together in the study group in New York City? I could never have managed that even with today's software. All unconsciously, behind the scenery of our lives, the choreography was being managed. Every single choice and turning point over those years moved us both inexorably toward each other to finally meet and recognize what we were to each other.

What is most interesting is that even when we did meet, we were not forced to marry. After all, both Ruth and I had other close friends, both women and men friends, but neither of us actually recognized any of them as life partners. No matter how intimate, the relationships never matured to a point where marriage illuminated the whole connection.

When I asked Ruth to marry me, I was taken by complete surprise. It had never occurred to me to marry anyone. I thought marriage was for other, older people, but not for me. How did I know that this was the person who would be the mother of the children we loved? How did it occur to me that marriage was the right thing?

When I look back at those times, I know now that angels must collaborate. Just as we humans develop agreements, help each other and work together on projects, so must the angels develop collaborative relationships?

My Angel certainly collaborated with Ruth's Angel. I can picture the two of them working together in harmony and spinning the threads of soul attractions out of the substances of time. As they worked together, Ruth and I each on our separate journeys gradually approached each other in New York. She was 25 years old and I was 22. That meant our angels had already associated with each other those many years, and as they became more and more connected, we in space traveled toward our meeting place.

Once we met, the next move was ours. Except! Our son Torin must also have an angel. Our son Mark has an angel. Long before they were born, their angels drew near to ours and were attracted by the wonderful project our angels were moving along. Between them all, in a sensitive space, Ruth and I and the children established our connections with each other to be fulfilled in a life.

Guess what, we were missing something. Ruth felt a girl was somehow part of our life. We met with attorneys, even paid fees and were ready to adopt, but nothing ever materialized. Then we thought maybe we could have a foster daughter and contacted an agency in Dobbs Ferry, New York. They interviewed us and began looking for a girl that we could include in our family on a foster basis. Months passed.

Finally a marvelous Mrs. Saad told us they had a little girl but her circumstances were such that she was not up for foster care. We were so disappointed, especially after Ruth actually visited and met the one-year-old girl.

"She is only up for adoption," Mrs. Saad explained sadly.

"But that's what we actually wanted," we both cried out.

"Why didn't you say so?"

"We tried for more than a year but could not find any little girl up for adoption."

"To tell you the truth, we never have children for adoption out of this agency, but this is a special situation that just happened to come along."

We decided to call her Angela because her Angel had to bring her along into our family by a special unusual route.

Isn't it too bad that we can't actually see our angels with our eyes, and thank them for all they arrange without our knowing it! Maybe we couldn't handle it. Maybe it is a good thing we don't see them and have to actually look for them in our lives and biographies, leaving their gentle and sometimes not so gentle footprints as events and turning points. Creating a biography is hard work and we can use all the help we can get. Our angels collaborate with each other and with us to form a life's biography in keeping with the laws of the soul.

I now know that, as long as one looks at one's own biography from the beginning to current events, from earlier to later, each moment seems to follow the previous moment very rationally and logically. We conclude that life is somewhat like our thinking, namely that there is no meaningful relationship between a moment in the past and a moment that follows it in the future. The only relationship is that it is next in line. As a result a biography becomes a sequence of curious facts. Life becomes a kind of mechanical clockwork.

However, if we dare to look at our biography from a later point back to an earlier one, we are struck differently by what we see. It seems as though earlier phases only become meaningful when viewed from the perspective of a later phase.

A student goes through his pre-medical education at a University and then undergoes medical training and then serves as an intern in a hospital. He is driven by a vision of himself as a doctor. He suffers immensely to achieve a goal he cherishes. Eventually he opens his practice where he believes he can best serve. Looking forward from the day he first enters college, every step of the way seems linear, open at every point to take a different direction, quite pushed from behind as though the cause of each later point is to be found in the earlier one. Cause and effect form a chain lugubriously lurching into an unknown future.

Looking at the same chain from the day he opens his practice, or more likely buys a practice or joins an existing practice, and looking back toward his first attending college our perspective shifts. Was the cause of the entire chain the becoming a doctor and practicing medicine, and all the effects of that cause were to be found in the enrolling in college, premed, medical school and internship?

No doubt we humans can look at it either way, because we are so anchored in space and see time as a kind of mechanical sequencing of events. But suppose we were able to oversee time and blend before and after into a meaningful whole, would we then begin to comprehend how our angels work and collaborate?

If I had not just finished my short story and felt reluctant to get on with the editing, would everything that followed been different? Suppose the Daily News had a lulu of a story to cover, would I then have had to go to work and not been able to go to the study group? Suppose I didn't just feel like a walk, felt unsure of what to do with a whole evening stretching before me and not ending up at Columbus Circle? (Incidentally, I rarely walked in that direction. I usually walked north on Broadway, not south.) I had no intention of dropping in on the study group, but I did. Did I have a good reason? Did I usually do what my mother asked me to do? Guess again! I cannot explain why I went. And if I had not gone, I would not have met Ruth, and think how that would have changed the next 60 years or even longer, given the influence our children and grandchildren have and will have on the growing movement of environmental and social sustainability.

The other way to look at it is to say that Ruth and I meeting was a necessity that caused all the earlier events leading up to the actual cause, the meeting.

I struggle with these thoughts because my Angel living in time probably oversees the future, the present and the past. She probably sees a panoramic collage opening limitless points of interest to Angel inquiry and unlimited number of possibilities to draw near and collaborate. A space being and a time being join forces to create the music called biography and history. I so wish historians would look at history backward with hindsight and draw conclusions from the angel perspective.

23

FIFTH CONCLUSIONS ABOUT ANGEL BEHAVIOR

My Angel apparently could influence what came to meet me in the course of my life, but she was not allowed to interfere or even to command or order me to act in certain ways. She had to leave me in charge of my decisions and actions. Most of the time when she was involved certain ideas came to me, not compulsively but just suggestively. I would suddenly have an idea to walk toward downtown Manhattan. I had no particular reason, it just came to me, somewhere between an attractive idea and an impulse to do something. I knew I had not manufactured the thought. It came to me more from the outside, but somehow connected with my feelings.

That's another rule it seemed. Every such idea or impulse stirred up feelings in me. My feelings were a kind of filter, filtering out unsuitable ideas and urging me to act when the thought and the feeling were compatible. The Angel only had access to my thought world, never directly to my feelings or will. The rule seemed to be that whatever I willed was my responsibility, but she had to suffer the consequences with me. Whatever I thought, even with great effort, ultimately seemed only an appeal to my Angel which she responded to or not as was her nature. After some years I began to notice that the approach of my Angel always summoned an idea or an impulse. I began to think some of my ideas were actually simply transformed angel activity. I had no direct access to such angel activity, but it simply transformed into an idea or an impulse as it reached me.

What if an idea was actually independent of me, came to me as a disguised angel? What if I was organized as a human to be blind to angels but could sense them as ideas only? Could ideas be the garment of angels? Could it be that our human condition blinded us to angels but allowed us to sense their proximity in the form of an idea? What if every thought was nothing less than the appearance of an angel disguised as a thought. That meant the angel left us our freedom, since a thought was never compulsive. The angel that way had no power over us that we ourselves did not accept. We are currently so organized that we can either accept an idea or reject it. That gives us the possibility of freedom from higher beings, or perhaps even lower beings, whomever they may be. After all, not all our thoughts are commendable even in our eyes!

If so, that would mean that angels were not always fluffy and sweet and beautiful, since ideas were not always fluffy and sweet and beautiful. Of course we humans would be the translators and maybe a lot gets lost in translation, if I may borrow the thought. Nevertheless I won through to the concept that angels were just as varied and differentially unique as humans. In a way we humans could be looked at as a mirror image of an angel society, struggling and associating with each other, leaving us with the consequences of their interactions, translated into ideas and impulses that we proudly think of as our own. There's a thought worth considering. A dual social field in which angels and humans interacted causing the multiplicity of actions and motivated impulses we know as history. Instead of history, "his story," it should be called "ourstory."

I reasoned that angels cause ideas to surface in three different ways. One way was in response to our inner activity we call thinking. It's a strain to think when confronted with a problem or question. The strain we feel is felt by the angel as a kind of invitation to get involved. As the angel approaches, is engaged, we light up with an idea or impulse. Depending on the maturity of the angel, the idea is useful, right or beneficial to humanity, or it can be useless, wrong or harmful to others. It depends on the maturity of the angel but also on our ability to translate the angel activity. We are mutually responsible for the nature of the idea, even though we alone are responsible for what we do with it.

The second way, I learned, for an angel to influence our thought world was through our instinctive impulses. The angel makes use of what appears to us as not very important. Perhaps we have nothing very important to do and are wandering down the street when we decide for no apparent reason to cross to the other side. I know Freud would have a heyday with this, but I have frequently sensed the presence of my Angel in such impulsive decisions. Apparently unimportant, the angel seizes it and transforms it into something meaningful for our lives.

The third way my Angel influences me is to meddle in my sleep. How often have I woken up in the morning with either a definite feeling of something I need to do, or else the suggested action for a problem or question I went to sleep with the night before. At least in my case, I seem to be more susceptible to angel activity during my sleep than when I am awake. So much the better for me and hallelujah for the sanctity of sleep.

SECTION FOUR

ANGEL CHOREOGRAPHY

"When an angel is active, subsequent events are the real causes of earlier effects in time. The angel must experience time, past and future, as a whole, intricate movement, culminating in the present moment."

24

Episode 16: Finding a Profession

It seemed quite natural to accept the job at the Rudolf Steiner School in New York City. After a number of years consisting of kindergartens and grades one to eight, the school had decided to expand grade by grade into the high school years.

Since it was the very first ninth grade for the school, the eighth grade students would be pioneering not only the ninth grade but all the way to graduation four years later. It took considerable courage for the parents of those students to enroll them, somewhat reluctantly, in the ninth grade.

"We want football," the six boys insisted.

"Why?" I wanted to understand.

"Everybody else does it. Every school plays football. We see them in the park. They clunk by us in their cleats, their shoulders built out and their helmets under their arms. They look great!"

"How many of you have played football before?"

"You mean tackle?"

"Yes."

Not one of them raised their hands.

"It will take some time to get into shape. Maybe this first year we could use another sport, like European football, to work ourselves up in skill and muscle power to have the makings of a team by next year. It will be hard work. Every day after school we'll need to run and exercise hard. We'll need nine good players to have any kind of a game with another team. Do you really want that and are you ready for all that's involved to get in shape?"

That seemed to appeal to them. They knew that at least eleven players were necessary for football, while in soccer only nine would make a team. The eighth grade behind them had a few larger boys and could be helpful as substitutes.

That is how I began teaching at the Rudolf Steiner School in New York City. Naturally, basketball and baseball followed for the other seasons, and teaching English as the grades expanded into the high school complemented sports and physical education. The idea of football never surfaced again, and four years later, when that class graduated, the team had a winning season that pleased everyone.

After that I needed to teach a sixth grade of wonderful students as their class teacher, taking the place of their earlier teacher who contracted cancer and could not continue. Another turning point approached. As always, a turning point has signs leading up to it. The earliest sign was after a class meeting for the fathers, which I had called.

"Something is happening in my class. I have called you, the fathers, here this evening to describe what I see going on and to ask for your help. Up to now, the class has been a harmonious mini society. True, we have had challenges, but we always pulled together, boys and girls alike, and we were able to deal with all problems affably.

About two weeks ago I became aware of a change. Something was creeping into our class that does not seem serious, but maybe needs us to heighten our awareness. One of the boys would stick out a foot as a girl would walk forward to the blackboard. The girl did not fall, she jumped aside ably and went on her way. One of the girls was somewhat tearful as she shared with the other girls that a boy had pulled her pigtails so hard it still felt sore. I noticed during recess that the clusters of students in the class had shifted. There seemed to be boy–boy clusters and girl–girl clusters, whereas up to now there were only mixed groups.

I am wondering what our sons think it is to be "manly." I wonder whether we are paying attention to what is happening both here and at home and if there is something we should be doing about it? That's what I wanted to ask you and I have asked Dr. Pensalatus to describe a little of what is going on physically in girls and boys of this age as a start to the conversation."

There followed the most interesting conversation about growing up, about manliness and "being a lady." We were all just fathers, men, and shared many thoughts and feelings on the subject.

By 8:30 p.m. the meeting drew to a close and one of the fathers suggested in a kind of camaraderie that we all pop in at the Crystal Coffee Shop around the corner and have some refreshment. They urged me to come along.

Once in the coffee shop and served, they all chatted informally with each other and ignored me. They talked about their work and professions. I heard descriptions of market research projects, architectural drawings and problems with zoning and permitting. I heard about financial analysis, investing, business ethics and legal issues. A whole world opened up for me as I listened. I realized I knew almost nothing about that world; even the terminology was foreign to me. I was on the sidelines of professions, which dominated the lives of these men, and I knew nothing about them.

Somewhere a humming began in me. It felt a little like a wish to find out more, a desire to enter into that world and experience its laws and forces. I did not form any resolution at that moment, but from then on I harbored something in my soul that would undoubtedly have an effect.

Shortly thereafter the administration of the school decided that salaries would be reviewed and that all teachers should examine their budgets to see whether the school was meeting the needs of each teacher. It was a wish to pay according to need and not so much according to merit or even time worked. The idea was to find out what each person needed.

Ruth and I were both idealists. We struggled together putting down on paper every item of expenditure in our monthly budget. Then we reviewed each item to decide whether it was really necessary or whether we could do without. Ruth thought she could take in one or two other preschool children during the day since she already had one child to take care of. She also thought she could bake more loaves of her healthy bread since other mothers were asking her for it. We worked out what to charge and included that in the budget as additional income. When all was finished and we could not scrap another penny, we arrived at the total of $6,500 as the annual total, which we would need to exist in New York City at that time (1962). I placed our calculations in an envelope and turned it into the treasurer.

Some time later the treasurer asked to meet with me. He had my budget paper in his hand as we talked. He asked a few questions about some of the items and I answered them candidly.

At last, he sighed, spread his hands in a wide gesture as if in resignation and said, "I have gone over all the budgets of teachers and staff. As you might imagine, the total far exceeds our income as a school. I then took the income and spread it across the board and came up with a number for each salaried person."

"I see."

"That number for you comes to $6,000, which is actually all the school can afford to pay you," he continued.

For a moment I was stunned, not knowing what to say and not sure how to respond. Finally I tried to express my thoughts.

"Ruth and I struggled for several evenings to calculate the smallest amount that we would need to survive. We eliminated all luxuries, all entertainment, and even some medical expenses that might come up during the year. We eliminated everything except the bare bones necessities; $6,500 is the smallest number we came up with for our survival. You are asking me to live on less than the minimum? I have no savings, no parents or grandparents to beg for funds. Ruth already contributes bread money and baby-sitting money to the budget we have drawn up. How do you picture us living on less than we need?"

Again he spread his hands wide to indicate helplessness on his part. "There is only so much money and I cannot squeeze out more than there is. $6,000 is all the school can manage."

"In other words, you do not care whether we survive or not. That's my problem?"

"We care a great deal, but are limited in what is available and if we did not pay attention to our limits, the school would go into deficit, start borrowing and end up having to close."

"But that's what you are asking me to do."

"As treasurer, I have to look out for the school!"

"As father and husband, I have to look out for my family."

I was wounded. Money was sharpening my consciousness and making me face up to my own personal responsibilities for the first time in my life. I was 28 years old and many would say it was about time. I grew up always managing to exist without worrying about money. Now all of a sudden it seemed I was expected to look out for myself. Not only that but it seemed it was part of the equipment an adult was supposed to have. Looking out for oneself was honorable and mature. For the first time in my life I considered putting my own needs in the center of my consciousness and letting everyone else worry about their own needs.

Without thinking through all the consequences, I indicated to the school that I would no longer continue as an employee at the conclusion of the school year.

"What ever will you do?" a member of the College of Teachers asked me, worry showing in every line on her brow.

"Look out for myself, as I am forced to do. The world has abandoned me and now I will use the world to provide for my family and myself. Isn't that the grown-up thing to do?" I asked with, I think, just a touch of bitterness in my voice.

The teacher looked at me, not understanding what had gotten into me. "But...," she began.

"Life goes on, and we'll manage," I comforted her.

"What are we going to do?" I asked Ruth at home.

Ruth put our son Torin to bed, arranged the apartment where we lived and assumed that was a good enough answer.

"I will look for a job. No doubt something will turn up."

"No doubt," she said wonderingly.

The next day I began working on a resume and a sales pitch. Then I began cutting out ads in newspapers and answering them. In the meantime I finished out the school year, bid farewell to my class and watched them spill out of the school into their summer vacation. I was sure they would be fine. They were a strong bunch, full of courage and energy. They would be fine!

All of June I answered ads and talked my way through interviews without any success. Part of the problem was that I didn't know

Episode 16: Finding a Profession

what to look for. Teaching was behind me, neatly packaged into my biography. I wanted something else, something totally new that still made use of my capacities. But what was that? Teaching was out. I didn't really care for administrative work in schools. Manual labor or sales didn't lure me. What was there in the world that needed me and was made to order for my talents and ambitions?

"How much money have you got left?" I asked Ruth.

"Nothing." She answered too lightly.

" I have some quarters in my pocket."

"Let's go down to Schraffts and have a fudge sundae together," Ruth suggested helpfully.

"Good idea!" I think she was surprised, but as always she was game to the last, full of confidence and trust in the world and what it had in store for us.

We sat together in Schraffts at the counter and shared a fudge sundae with whipped cream on top, using two spoons and alternating until it was finished.

Now, I knew I had to make something happen. Our back was against the wall. It was very motivating. I was up early the next morning and talked my way through an interview that went nowhere. I had no real appetite for the job and the interviewer had no appetite for me. We went through the motions and ended pleasantly enough.

"Why don't you try teaching?" she suggested.

"I did."

I wandered out on Madison Avenue, walked a few blocks and began to feel the weight of the world settle on my shoulders. I had forgotten all about my Angel and wasn't listening!

At the corner of Madison Avenue and 49th Street I paused. A red light stopped me. Since I was walking aimlessly, I could have turned and taken advantage of the green light crossing Madison, but instead I just waited almost listlessly for the light to change. Beside me was the light post and I leaned against it. Beside the post there was one of those wire wastebaskets the city used for collecting trash of all kinds. I glanced into it as though it were a likely place for finding hope and consolation.

A folded newspaper was on top of the trash. It showed the picture of a bald man pointing his finger out at me, a ferocious expression on his face, not at all friendly like Uncle Sam promising a career to young recruits. The headline on the ad was equally aggressive. The ad demanded, "Young ambitious men WANTED!" I almost turned away, a queasy feeling in my stomach. Something was gnawing at me. I turned and looked again at the advertisement. It offered a lucrative career with opportunities for advancement and success, but only for hardworking aggressive individuals. I read on. It seemed the career involved being an advisor to businesses and other organizations, doing research and planning as well as building up a portfolio of clients.

I looked at the address of the George S. May Company. The company was located in a suite only blocks from where I stood. I grabbed the newspaper and strode down Madison Avenue to meet who knows what. A sense of excitement welled up in me, which I could not entirely explain. How was I to know that the rest of my life was beckoning me from a newspaper ad? Who could have guessed?

When I entered the Suite, its luxurious furniture impressed me as did the model sitting behind the reception desk talking into her phone.

"Can I help you?" she wondered.

Episode 16: *Finding a Profession*

"I read your ad in the Mirror and would like to ask some more questions about the interesting career it offers someone like me."

"Please have a seat."

"Thank you."

She seemed disappointed when she returned. Her expression offered no hope.

"Mr. May will not see you until you have taken our test."

"What kind of test?" I asked.

"It looks like this!" She waved a booklet at me.

"Does it take more than an hour?" I asked smiling.

"That depends on you," she laughed. I knew she liked me, which was a good omen. Maybe she did the grading!

"Can I take it now?"

"That's the idea."

She led the way into a small conference room. I took off my jacket, hung it over the back of the chair, sat down and looked at the test.

"Is there a time limit?" I asked.

"Five o'clock," she said. "That's when I go home."

It was my turn to laugh. I turned the first page and leafed quickly through all the pages, as was my way of becoming familiar with any test I took. There was no doubt what the test was interested to find out. All the questions were similar. If I entered late into a lecture hall and the lecturer had already started, would I go to the front of the room and take the empty seat in the front row or slip quietly into the empty seat in the back row. The only smart thing to say was clear to me at once.

I finished the test in record time. I needed no time for introspection. Occasionally I wondered whatever happened to such qualities as sensitivity, empathy and thoughtfulness. Aggressiveness seemed king and I gave the George S. May Company what they wanted.

"Wow!" said Mr. May. "When can you start?"

"Is it too late to start today?"

"No. However you have to sign some papers, read over our manual and take the training program in the George S. May Program for Success. Our starting salary is $9,000, with all the benefits described in the little booklet I'm giving you. Can you be here at 9:00 a.m. tomorrow morning?"

"Sure." I remembered the five-minute training program of Barrett and Co. and felt reassured I would be earning money right away. "Can I ask you a few questions, first, before I sign anything?"

"I can see you are an intelligent fellow and want to be sure what you are getting yourself into. Go ahead, ask."

"What is the George S. May Program for Success?"

"Okay. The training program describes it in great detail but in short, it is an 8-step advisory process that enables any of our consultants to help a business to overcome its problems and improve its bottom line. You, as a George S. May Consultant, help the business to become more profitable."

"You mentioned an 8-step process that you teach your consultants?" I wondered.

"Yes," he agreed. "We teach you how to work up your consulting business from a $1,000 start-up to $100,000."

"I don't understand" was my response.

"Let's say you are somewhat familiar with the restaurant business, okay?" He started to get quite animated. "We'll use that as an example! Let's just say I happen to know from your resume that restaurant management is one of your fields of expertise. Restaurants are one of the businesses you get to call on. We teach you how to sell an initial assignment that looks at all the various aspects of the restaurant business for a mere $1,000 to identify the three or four areas of improvement that could increase their profitability. You make a convincing case for looking more deeply into one of those areas for $3,000. You show them that the increase in profitability would far exceed the cost of the study. Do you get the idea?"

"In other words, they pay me $1,000 to identify an area of improvement, and then $3,000 to show them how," I summarized.

"Exactly." He beamed at me triumphantly.

"How?" I asked.

"How?" He seemed puzzled. "How what?"

"That's what I want to know. How do I improve their business?"

"I am sure you can figure that out. A bright fellow like you!" he encouraged me. "Anyway, the George S. May Program for Success will show you, step by step, how you take any business from an initial assignment for $1,000 to a final assignment of $100,000. All it takes is determination, desire to succeed and the George S. May Program of Success. I am sure that together we will be a great success and you, young man, will earn a great deal of money!"

"It sounds very encouraging," I ventured.

"So it is. Just sign here and show up tomorrow morning at 9:00 a.m."

Mr. May pushed a single sheet of paper toward my end of his desk.

"What am I signing?" I asked innocently.

"This offers you the job of consultant. It specifies a starting salary of $9,000 and lists the benefits provided by the George S. May Company. It further stipulates that the George S. May Company requires you to enroll in its training program beginning tomorrow morning at 9:00 a.m. Should you not show up for any reason, our offer expires and becomes null and void. Your signature indicates agreement to these terms." He smiled at me.

I signed, we shook hands across the desk and I left.

"See you bright and early." He cheered me out.

I stood on the street corner for a minute, thinking hard. $9,000 sounded very good, and they obviously expect something from me or they would not pay me $9,000. I was receiving little warning bells that didn't give me a clue what was wrong. I wasn't afraid to sell. I had done that before, selling Bibles. Is that what I wanted to do all over again?

The idea of advising businesses and helping them improve their operations and their profitability was deeply appealing. That would be something new. Did I know anything about how to improve a business? Reluctantly, I admitted my ignorance. I wondered if there really was such a profession.

I was only a few blocks from the New York Public Library, which covered a whole city block at 42nd street. I moved rapidly down the few blocks, intervening, and found myself at the main desk of the library.

"I want to find out if there is such a profession called "consultant," I said to the pleasant clerk behind the desk. She looked at me astonished over the rims of her glasses.

"Where have you been all these years?" she asked. "I get it!" She then laughed. "You're joshing me."

"I've been teaching children."

"Even so, you should have read the newspapers once in a while and seen the ads at least."

"Well, I take it there is such a profession!"

"Look," she said kindly. "Go over there to the telephone book and look up the phone number of the Association of Management Consulting Engineers. That should get you started on catching up with the present century."

"I'm not an engineer."

"That's just what they call it. Good luck." She moved off to check out some books for a man in a business suit. I thought of asking him, since he looked quite professional, then thought better of it and found my way to the telephone books stacked in an accessible shelf near the front of a long table, at which sat people hunched over, silent and inaccessible.

There it was. Association of Management Consulting Engineers. I wrote down the phone number on the back of a receipt and left. A bank of pay phones outside the library had one that was free, which I grabbed. I inserted a quarter and waited.

"Hello?" was the answer.

"My name is Finser. I have been teaching, and I heard about the profession of consulting and became so interested in it that I applied for a job with the George S. May Company. Now I am not sure I am doing the right thing and need someone to talk with about consulting. Any chance I can talk with you?" It all spilled out before I knew what I was doing. Whoever had answered was speechless.

"Hello?" I asked.

"Yes, I am here. Do you want to come over right now?"

"Yes. Can you tell me something about the George S. May Company?"

"Not over the phone. Why don't you get over here, and I'll be glad to share whatever I know in person." He gave me the address and hung up.

Again, it was just around the corner. Every place I needed to be seemed in close proximity. It almost seemed someone had clustered everything I needed for easy access.

Philip Shay was lodged in a one-room office piled with magazines and books. His friendly face looked at me curiously from under a light-brown shock of hair that was only loosely combed. He might have been a professor at a community college. He did wear a tie and a tweed sport jacket.

"Now tell me your story. Over the phone it seemed a bit abridged to give me any real knowledge of what you are all about."

I then told him about my teaching at the Rudolf Steiner School, my other various experiences and how I answered the ad. He laughed. "So what do you think about the job?" he wanted to know.

"Well, the idea of helping businesses improve their operations and becoming more profitable is very appealing. Even though I have no experience doing it, I would really love to learn. The George S. May Company seems mostly interested in aggressively selling their services rather than actually helping the client businesses. This may not matter very much, but I also have a strange feeling in my gut that something is not right, but I don't know exactly what."

"What I am going to say you never heard here, and I will deny that I ever said it."

"Okay, I understand."

"From all that I have heard, that employer will hire any bright, ambitious young man as consultant to drum up business for the company. I don't know of anyone who lasted very long there, and I am not sure how much good they ever did a potential client. If I were in your shoes, I would reconsider starting your career there."

"I see. I am sorry to hear that. Not just because it was a job paying $9,000, but because the idea of advising businesses and helping them to improve seems so appealing. I would love to learn how to do that and do it well."

"You'll probably not learn that at the George S. May Company. If you want to get into consulting, find a reputable firm and apply to them for a job. There are literally hundreds of reputable consulting firms all over the country, especially in New York and all along up to Boston, even into Canada. You'll have no trouble finding good reputable firms all up and down the East Coast," he suggested helpfully.

"Yes. I think I'll do that. I am a quick learner and do not shirk hard work. Whatever company hires me will be lucky and pleased with the results."

"I tell you what," Philip volunteered. "Why don't you pop right over to Barrington & Company, a smaller consulting firm right across the street from here that has just landed a consulting assignment in Rochester, New York. It is an organizational planning study for the Rochester School System, and they do not have a single consultant who has ever worked in education. Who knows, they might benefit by having someone on board with an educational background."

"Great, it's worth a try."

"Ask for Ted Tullin. He's a friend and I think the two of you will get along." Philip Shay then offered, "I'll give him a heads-up that you're on the way."

"Thanks."

Philip Shay had scratched the company name, address and Ted Tullin on a piece of paper, which I held in my hand as I crossed the street and found my way up to the 7th floor of the Graybar Building.

Ted Tullin came out to the reception to meet me and escort me back to his office. We talked a while. I was very honest and admitted I knew nothing about consulting, but was very familiar with education and teaching. Since I had also served on the College of Teachers at the Rudolf Steiner School, I also knew a little about school administration.

The assignment for the Rochester School District had two parts to it. One part was an organization study to recommend a more efficient organization for the school district. That part of the assignment would be carried by one of the senior consultants who had experience in that area.

"The other part of the assignment is a salary and classification study to design the compensation system involving all staff positions, as well as teaching and educational management positions. There's where I think you could fit it. It requires meetings with principals, assistant principals, department heads and teachers. It may even include the design of a teacher-performance program that will probably have to be ratified by the teachers," Ted explained to me.

"That sounds exciting, and I can't wait to start," was all I could manage to say.

"Wait just a second. You'll have to meet the VP in charge of this division, and then we'll need to fill out some papers and sign an employment agreement," Ted cautioned.

A few minutes later, I met Vin Wilking, my boss and mentor for the next four years. We got along instantly. I looked up to him with awe and affection. He was incredibly skilled in dealing with potential clients, selling assignments and performing the work. What I learned from him is priceless. We were on the road quite a bit, which meant long car rides, airplane trips, even some unscheduled airport layovers. Vin never ceased to entertain me with stories of assignments and problems he had solved.

He also generously admitted his family problems, which he called his massive private payroll. He was struggling with his third wife and astounded me with episodes where he was locked out of his own house and how he dealt with all these problems.

The first time we had dinner together on the road, he ordered a martini and offered me one. I had never had any hard liquor before. An occasional beer and even a sherry or sweet vermouth was the extent of my experience. I thought I could allow myself one, since I had become such an important and world-wise consultant. By the end of the meal, I had nearly slipped under the table. Vin had a few more and then switched to scotch. I have never seen it, but others told me he managed a whole bottle of scotch on occasion and never missed a beat in the discussion or conversation with clients. He became increasingly brilliant as others began to droop and confuse their syllables.

I have often found that the most worthwhile individuals, even great ones with purpose and mission in their blood, have a glaring fault or weakness as companion to their brightness. I wonder whether perfection in humans is at all like perfection in mathematics or in Christology. A perfect crystal can be admired and cherished but rarely loved, while often a human being without a single flaw is not loved. We humans seem to expect one or two flaws in one another, laugh about them even, and usually mention them with affectionate humor.

I admired Vin and appreciated him almost as a father I never knew. He gave so freely of his wisdom and experience. He never tried to lord it over me with his singular talent. Often, he let me carry the ball in conversations, pitching in when it was wanted and needed, listening intently, almost as if he were looking for pointers himself. The next four years gave me what I needed to be an effective organizational advisor.

The first assignment for the Rochester school system also brought me under the tutelage of Wilbur K. Williams, the division head for all salary and classification studies. He taught me how to follow, step by step, the process of designing a compensation system based on a number of irrefutable factors, interviews that lead to job descriptions, evaluating and aligning each job grouped into classes, and finally relating the compensation levels of each class with market data gathered in an external survey.

The most difficult part of the assignment was often to deal with the jobs that had more of a political significance than task significance. That's when I was called upon to be creative and use all of my imaginative capacities. Often I was able to reveal surprising elements of a job not even realized by the incumbent through some creative writing and thinking.

I am so grateful for having this opportunity to find a profession that would employ every bit of talent and capacity I could muster. I felt so grateful at the time that a few days after being hired by Barrington & Company, I called the Association of Management Consulting Engineers to thank Philip Shay.

"Who?" the strange voice on the line asked.

"Philip Shay."

"Oh!" There were a few awkward moments of silence and then some whispering I could not make out. "Mr. Shay no longer works for the association. I'm sorry."

"Really?" It was a complete surprise for me. "Do you know where I can reach him?"

"No, I'm sorry. I can't help you." She hung up abruptly.

As for Ted Tulin, shortly after hiring me he resigned to open a hardware store in Ridgefield, New Jersey. Barrington & Company lasted a few years, and then went out of business, selling its personnel division to W. K. Williams, who carried on with what he knew best for many years.

Isn't it wonderful that Philip Shay was in the job as executive director of the Association of Management Consulting Engineers for exactly the amount of time it took for me to find out about consulting, and just when I needed his help?

How wonderful that Ted Tulin was there to guide me into the company and connect me with Wilbur K. Williams and Vin Wilking, the two men who would have the most influence on my consulting style. Imagine if they had not just happened to be there for my benefit.

Barrington & Company was already showing some signs of difficulty. Most of the junior consultants like myself were 80% to 90% chargeable to clients, but the senior staff, of whom there were probably a few too many, were not chargeable for even 40% to 50% of their time. This meant that the most costly resource was running the company into a hole, while the fees earned by charging the junior staff to clients could not compensate for the red ink.

I was very grateful that Barrington & Company existed long enough to hire me, teach me and give me enough experience to launch me further into a career in a profession that fitted me like a glove. I sometimes list the sequence of happenstance that seemed too good to be totally accidental:

1. Spending our last change on a fudge Sundae, putting me squarely against the wall for the next day's search activity.
2. Finding myself discouraged and confused on the corner of Madison Avenue, possibly waiting for the red light to change

to green. Maybe the red light in my life was also on the verge of changing to green.

3. Having those few seconds of listlessness and letting my eyes fall into the wastebasket on the corner.
4. The obnoxious advertisement in the folded newspaper irritated and then drew me toward the George S. May Company.
5. The false connection with Mr. May, the sharpening of my instincts and warning alerts sounding through every fiber of my being, and still pushing me on to where I needed to be.
6. The charming librarian at the New York Public Library and her terse advise to look in the phone book for the Association of Management Consulting Engineers. What a novel idea!
7. The contact with Philip Shay, timed for the narrow window of his employment at the association.
8. The friendly connection between Philip Shay and Ted Tulin, without which I might not have been able to slip in without an appointment and without credentials.
9. The warm connection with Ted Tulin, who was just there long enough to get me into the company before finally realizing his cherished dream of owning and running a hardware store in Ridgefield, New Jersey. What kept him lingering at Barrington & Company for my arrival?
10. The eventual demise of Barrington & Company, but not before it provided me with the most outstanding training and experience in the conduct of orderly practical research projects in real time.

25

Commentary about Angel Footprints

Now, when I had time to think about it, I began to feel really lucky. Wasn't it lucky that I stopped at the red light and looked into the wastebasket on Madison Avenue? Wasn't it lucky that the newspaper just happened to be open to the page showing the advertisement of the George S. May Company? How amazing that I was attracted to the idea of advising companies, the profession I carried for the rest of my life. Wasn't it fortuitous that the librarian at the New York Public Library happened to know about consulting and was helpful enough for me to locate the Association of Management Consulting Engineers? What a stroke of luck that Philip Shay was on the job and feeling kindly toward me, enough to help me connect with Ted Tulin. Just imagine if Ted had decided to leave Barrington & Company a few weeks earlier and not been there as a friend of Philip Shay to look favorably on my employment.

It seemed to me that I had a day during which I slid along a greased pathway of happenstance and coincidence to a goal I hadn't planned, yet was precisely appropriate for my next step in life.

Never before had I experienced such a smooth slide from one life condition to another. Never before had I spent my last bit of change, and the next day would bring a salary of $9,000—$3,000 more than I had been earning as a teacher at the Rudolf Steiner School.

All I had learned as a teacher complemented what I learned now as a consultant. The people skills, the ability to "wing it." When necessary, the confidence and poise that one can only acquire in front of children, the ability to think on one's feet as needed. These all were initially developed in the classroom.

The ability to bring logic and sequence to facts and points were learned in consulting. Also learned were the ability to form presentations while also maintaining human contact and flexibility to responses from an audience. The idea that facts need to be the basis of a recommendation was also honed in those early consulting years.

Have I gone back far enough? What was the connection between my financial disagreements with the treasurer of the Rudolf Steiner School and my eventual move? How did my evening with the fathers of the children in my class factor into the sequence? The series of events was not a chain with each link visibly connected with the subsequent ones, it was more like ground water that bubbled up into the greenery on the surface at significant moments. Now looking back on the whole sequence I felt the underlying connected movement as though delicately managed for my benefit.

A wisdom far greater than mine was at work leaving footprints all over the sequence of events that eased me into the next chapter of my life.

Yes, I had forgotten my Angel for a while, but her footprints were everywhere I looked. Was I so important that she should devote so much time and energy to my biography? Perhaps I was really important to her. Maybe I should be achieving something really worthwhile and all these events and happenings were a preparation, a schooling to get me in shape for something important. Sure, I was far less than perfect, but if in the end I could accomplish what we both needed to achieve, does it matter that I am imperfect? Who cares, as long as we can both develop further together?

I began to look forward to a future in which what I was intended to accomplish seemed to be lurking.

SECTION FIVE

AMONG THE MIGHTY AND POWERFUL

"There is only a very thin line between knowledge and faith. Knowledge can move us ever closer to what we believe."

26

Episode 17: All about Power

Harold Geneen was piecing together a $10 billion conglomerate. He believed only the very best people, the smartest and most ambitious people, could fulfill his intentions for ITT. At its peak, the personnel department swelled its ranks to as many as 350 people.

Harold Geneen's idea was that a corporation with a presence in every major country of the world and in every major industry could survive any political or natural crisis. There would always be another country or another industry that would be profiting from the ill fortune. He also believed that the best carefully prepared executives could be parachuted into any company regardless of industry or culture and land ready to function fully. He wanted, above all, to instill in every executive and every employee for that matter a love for the facts. He used every management meeting to train his cadre of exceptional executives in how to distinguish between an opinion and a fact.

Once every month, the top staff would gather for an entire week in the huge conference room to review the operational results of every ITT-acquired company in the world. Each acquired company president and top staff would assemble on one side of the large oblong circle of tables. All the relevant numbers would be projected onto three large screens on the three sides opposite where Geneen and the two other members of the Office of the President would sit.

The meeting was supposed to start at 9:00 a.m., but we all knew it could start at any time. Many of us connected with our counterparts and discussed various business and non-business issues of interest, waiting for the meeting to begin. Sometimes another member of the office of the president would question some items on the agenda, but we all knew nothing important was going on.

Most of the seats around the tables were empty. In the next room, loaded with varied non-alcoholic refreshments, a few clusters and pairs of executives also caught up on news and the latest events. The clock on the wall crept slowly toward 10:00 a.m., and then toward 10:30.

Quite unexpectedly, a rustle of sound spread through the large spaces, and turning toward the conference room it was surprising to see every chair occupied as Harold Geneen swept into his seat on the long side of the oval, immediately starting the meeting. How everyone knew he was coming and would be there shortly is a mystery only known by the psyche of ITT. I don't even know how I knew. I just felt it and knew.

Geneen was relentless when he bore into a problem for which an answer was not evident at once. On one side of the room sat the president, the vice presidents and anyone else that might provide information about the subsidiary corporation. On the near side sat Geneen, the two other members of the Office of the President, and then ranging on his left and right the top ITT corporate staff.

Sometimes if Geneen did not get an answer, one that satisfied him, he would pause, think a moment or two and then move in either of two directions. He might actually nod and move on to another question or even another subsidiary corporation. We all knew somebody had been let off the hook; somebody had been given a reprieve, at least on this round.

He might instead turn to one or another staff VP, either asking for an opinion or requesting the staff VP to look into a matter. It all sounded innocent enough, but we all knew that it meant a lack of confidence in the subsidiary management. It gave license to corporate staff to descend on the unhappy subsidiary and start asking for this and that. Rarely did a subsidiary president survive the onslaught. The staff dominated everyone's time and energy and prevented them from any possible problem solving of their own. The staff, on the other hand, did not want to get too identified with the problem in case it proved too difficult to solve. In particular, the North American staff earned the greatest amount of attention and credit by identifying the problem and highlighting it for corporate acknowledgement, not for solving anything.

My impossible job was to identify the most promising top executives, providing stimulating and complementary educational experiences preparing them for promotion and advancement within any country, industry, or industry group. I was fortunate to have as my immediate boss, Robert Braverman, an intelligent open-minded individual ready to try and risk almost anything. He helped me to assemble top-notch people for closed sessions in various locations around the world. Not only was he tremendously helpful, but he was also a good friend and enlivened many a walk in Brussels and London after a weekend of meetings.

ITT was not easy to get into. I ended up having twenty-three interviews. One of them in a corporate jet to Memphis. When I arrived for my interview at the World Headquarters on Park Avenue in Manhattan, he said, "Come along! We can talk on the way."

"On the way to where?"

"Memphis. This came up, and I've got to go. You don't mind, do you?"

The car downstairs took us to Tetterborough Airport in New Jersey. The jet then had another destination, so I was handed a ticket in Memphis to return home.

"How was the interview?" Ruth asked me.

"Guess what! I was interviewed at 32,000 feet. Maybe they wanted to see if I could stand the pressure?... I'm joking!" I said when Ruth seemed alarmed.

"Did it go well?"

"I did not goof, I think."

I did goof once. Bob Braverman had asked me what I thought of my boss at Xerox, which had acquired me along with Basic Systems. I told him the truth.

"Why do you do that?" he asked me curiously.

"What?"

"How do you know that Marty is not my good friend and that I admire him tremendously."

"You do?" I was shocked.

"I mean only how do you know! Why take such a big risk unnecessarily?"

"Well, now you know I'll tell you the truth. Isn't it good to get that hurtle behind us?"

I think that's why he hired me, and because none of the twenty-three interviews turned up really negative, except for one with whom no one else got along either.

One episode at a conference in southern Belgium is worth describing. It all began in New York at the world headquarters. What happened still astounds me. There was a rule at ITT that nobody dared to break. Anyone at any level of the organization could come and ask me questions or even make suggestions and comments. However, it had to be reported exactly the way it happened to one's immediate boss. That was the rule.

For several months I had been planning a conference at an isolated resort in southern Belgium. Eleven presidents of the European companies and a few of the Brussels and New York staffs, carefully selected to be open-minded and respectful of other opinions and cultures, were consulted and then invited. Bob Braverman and I would run the weekend conference. I had met ahead of time with each of the participants and learned from them what they considered to be important questions and issues. I wanted to create an atmosphere of trust so that the truth, what we really thought, could eventually emerge for all of us to share and hold in confidence.

Location and dates had already been informally agreed to with the participants. Before the formal invitations were sent and the attendance confirmed, I reviewed the plans again with the senior vice president of human resources, to whom I formally reported. I explained that we would gather in southern Belgium on Thursday for dinner and the first relaxed evening session, each sharing some biographical episodes as a kind of introduction to the weekend. The meetings would continue through Friday, including an evening session, and end on Saturday no later than 5:00 p.m., so that most participants could return home and spend Sunday with their families and to review privately what had happened over the weekend and acknowledge the individual relationships that had been furthered or inaugurated by the conference. My boss had some questions concerning how likely it was that something sensitive or politically dangerous might transpire, since these were all top executives around the office of the president, and nobody was there from that office to provide safeguards. He wondered whether one of them shouldn't attend.

I explained that it might inhibit free discussion and open sharing of feelings if someone were present who could summarily fire them the next day. My boss understood my point but seemed dubious about the event and what might be discussed that would be inhibited by a member of the office of the president. After all, they might fire one of them whether they were at the conference or not. Nevertheless, he gave me the point and left the attendance as it was planned.

The same afternoon, Jack Hanway, theoretically the head of all headquarters staff, dropped in to see my boss. They were behind a closed door for twenty minutes and Jack had gone when my boss called me in again.

"About the schedule for this conference," he began, "I don't think you should start on Thursday already. It takes two whole days out of the week when some very important people will be incommunicado. You add the Saturday and Sunday and you get four days when none of them are available. We think you should start on Friday evening and end Sunday around 5:00. They and you can all be back on the job Monday morning. These are all ambitious people and I know they want to take as little time out as possible. Trust me, I know this is a better plan."

I argued for a while since it ruined my plan and endangered the whole conference, but I said I would think about it.

I returned to my office and reviewed all the participants and their normal locations for travel and other considerations. I also looked at the calendar again and noticed that the weekend of the conference included Easter Sunday. I knew that for most of these particular participants this created a grave difficulty. I returned to my boss's office.

"I just looked over the calendar and it turns out the Sunday in question is Easter Sunday. That will certainly rule out going on through Sunday. We might even have trouble traveling and with reservations." I must have shown my pleasure at this turn of events.

"I don't see what that has to do with it. We don't stop functioning, and there have been many times when meetings were necessary over Easter and even some other holidays. Besides, this is a non-business, more personal type of gathering. It's not quite like working, I think. You go ahead and change the dates the way I told you, and we'll all be happy."

I returned to my office, steamed a while privately, and then called one or two of the participants to ask their opinion on such a change. They were horrified. Only one said he might not be able to attend. Two did not threaten me with that, but expressed their resentment, and I began to wonder how cooperative they might be, given their feelings about this change of date. I thought long and hard and then returned to my boss's office.

He started belligerently. "You're not back to tell me again that it's Easter Sunday, are you?" He was no doubt tired of the subject and thought he had settled it all an hour ago.

"No, not this time!" I spoke quietly, knowing full well what risks I was taking. "I've come to tell you that, in my opinion, the change of dates will undermine the effectiveness of the conference and may cause a great deal of resentment, which would work contrary to our intentions with it, and that it is a bad idea to shift the dates as you have suggested." He opened his mouth, but I went on somewhat more loudly before he could speak. "However, you are my boss and if you order me to change the dates against my best judgment, I will do what you order me to do."

He glared at me for a full minute without speaking, then he shrugged his shoulders and said, "No, you do what you think is best."

That was the end of that episode and cleared the way for the conference to continue as planned.

In this way I found out quite by accident how important it was to know exactly where the responsibility was lodged. Caving in to the semblance of power was a mistake if the responsibility was not also transferred. Executives in leading positions seem to learn as their career progresses how to get their own way without taking on the requisite responsibility. I found out this secret only by risking everything.

27

Episode 18: All about Powerlessness

We met just south of Liege at a quiet resort. ITT reserved the entire resort for the occasion.

The first evening began with a typical evening buffet meal that lasted till well after 9:00 p.m., including strong coffee, brandy and a few cigars. I was not sure where we were going, since most of the evening was taken up with the usual posturing, including some "I'm bigger than you" conversations. I should have expected this the first night. After all, it was the first time these executives had been together in one place, one room, getting close and personal. One or two didn't know what to say. They went into business affairs, and the whole crowd followed in great relief.

The next day, Saturday, went smoothly. We created a few topics and video-taped the conversation. Later, we reviewed portions of the tape, some revealing cultural characteristics that were easily admitted to and humorous.

After dinner, we adjourned to the lounge, and a quiet, relaxed mood descended on the gathering. We were comfortable with each other, had survived some more personal revelations and observed some cultural differences. No one could have guessed what happened next. It began innocently enough.

"You know, I have noticed that each of our companies here in Europe is different from the companies I have experienced in the

United States. I know it is not always smart to make generalizations, but maybe in this gathering I can mention my observation. Each of our companies has what I would call, for lack of a better word, a 'personality.' STC in England is not the same as SEL in Germany, even though both manufacture, install and operate telephone switching systems. Each has a personality unique to itself"

"I can attest to that," another volunteered. "I once had the opportunity to do some research at the company in Paris. I needed to interview about a dozen of their managers. They were all very cooperative. Each one took me to a different restaurant, equally fine, by the way. There must be thousands of excellent restaurants in Paris. After about six of these interviews, which were supposed to be scheduled for the early afternoon, but were usually delayed for one reason or another, I began to realize I was having a wonderful time, but I just wasn't getting the information I needed. It seemed my style of asking, or perhaps my asking at all, was not, how shall I say, priming the pump correctly? That's when it came home to me that the culture in the French company was different and needed a special touch."

"I think we all know what you're talking about. I know when we tried to accelerate the inventory calculations in SEL at the Stuttgart plant, we were met with a thousand objections and questions. We wondered whether they would ever accept the new methodology. After the third day, they finally agreed to switch over, not because we wanted them to, but because they saw it was better and wanted to convert. Two weeks later, mind you, two weeks later, they were on the new system. Once they saw its advantages, they made the conversion in their minds and implemented it pronto.

"On the other hand, when we visited STC just outside of London, they immediately saw its advantages and were completely willing to move on it. However, when we returned two months later, nothing had happened. There were still questions, unspoken and often related to whose job was affected and timing of approvals. I'm not sure to this day if I understand why it wasn't moving."

"Yes, it's something like that in our different companies here in Europe. Each one has a unique culture that isn't just a reflection of the president's personality. It's almost as though certain people belong to one company and not to another. I think U.S. companies are not so differentiated. The people are more interchangeable. They easily slip into a similar job in another company without any unhappiness or friction."

"If our companies have a soul, the employees have to be soul mates to get along. It's that deep in some cases. We rarely find our people skipping around through different companies in their career. Americans seem to move every three to five years, it seems."

"American companies are more mechanical than personal; at least, that's the way it seems to an outsider. They function more like machines. Our machines, generally speaking, seem to have a higher quality, but their human organizations are more mechanical."

"You know, sometimes I think about all of us and ITT. We are all a part of ITT, and yet in a way we are each unique and separate. I think of us all on a train, a freight train, with very individualistic cars being pulled along at a great tempo. Within each car, we are working very hard, making decisions, achieving outstanding results, each car like a beehive of activity and accomplishment. However, it's the driver up front that ultimately determines where we go. Who is that driver of ITT? It looks like it is Geneen, but he himself seems to be driven by some powers I don't fully comprehend. He's a little like a machine himself. Has anyone ever had a more personal, non-business conversation with him?"

"Yes, I have," another spoke up. "We were on a flight, sitting together, talking about business of course, but then there was a pause, a quiet moment. I thought maybe it would interest him to compare our lives with someone like Beethoven. I described Beethoven's life, his intensity, his music and going deaf, how he still seemed to hear it inside while continuing to compose the last several symphonies. I wanted to talk about our lives, when he turned his head to look at me. He looked right into my eyes, unblinking. He said not a word, but his eyes were so deeply puzzled and disturbed. It was as if he was saying to himself, 'Who is this creature? Where does he come from? Have I ever seen the likes of him before?' Then he resumed the business topic from before, and the moment passed as he settled into familiar territory."

They all laughed, familiar with similar personal experiences.

"What if we are all on this train, thinking there is some actual driver up front who knows where we are going. But what if we don't know who it is? What if the real driver is invisible and does not disclose his intention or plans? Maybe Geneen pulls the levers and works the gauges, but who laid the tracks for this train, and who is it that ultimately achieves our purposes? Will we know in our lifetimes or will future generations be asking us, 'Where the hell were you going?'"

"You think that's scary, but I sometimes wonder if maybe there is no one driving this train, and I might even question whether we are going anywhere. Maybe we are just circling, endlessly circling, viewing the same scenery, content with the familiar known, never finding the unknown?"

There was some thoughtful silence. Eighteen executives of a ten-billion-dollar corporation, growing at an astounding rate and gaining political and economic power, sat together late in an evening facing the unknown.

28

Episode 19: First Accident in Europe

It was 1970 and my success in Europe offered me a promotion too good to refuse in Brussels, Belgium at the ITT Europe, Africa and Middle East Headquarters. I settled my family in Krefeld, Germany, took an apartment in Brussels and commuted back and forth by train. I was only there two years before being promoted back to ITT headquarters in New York as Corporate Director of Executive Development. During those two years in Brussels, I was blessed with several good bosses, several wonderful colleagues, and interesting work.

My Angel decided to take a stronger hand in my further development. Whether it was because I was too slow, or because there was increasing urgency that I get up to snuff for a future assignment, I do not know. At any rate, I was given three outstanding lessons.

The president of STC in England asked me to run a weekend workshop for him and his top people. I agreed. Just before my trip, I began to develop a continuous thirst. Every time I drank one or two glasses of water or juice, I needed to urinate; of course, then I was thirsty again. This went on all through my travel from Krefeld, Germany, to London. By the time I reached STC, I was worried enough to ask for the company doctor, who quickly diagnosed my diabetic condition.

Diabetes is a condition at my age caused by a weakness in the pancreas. It cannot manufacture enough insulin to help the body convert the sugar in the blood into useful energy. As a result, the sugar levels climb in the blood and cause a kind of euphoria, or I would describe it as a queasy escape into never-never land. The doctor recommended that I check myself into a hospital when I returned to Krefeld and receive treatment. In the meantime, he gave me some pills to provide a little bit of control, with orders not to eat or drink anything sweet.

The workshop went well, and the president of STC was pleased. Although I facilitated the workshop, he was the star by design and, I think, to reflect the chief purpose of assembling for two days.

I returned to Krefeld, Germany, and put myself into the Krefeld General Hospital for diabetes. For two days, I ate only oatmeal and the sugar levels came down. I had a choice between two forms of treatment. The doctors explained that at my age, 37, and up to 40, it could be either juvenile diabetes or the old-age type. Juvenile diabetes is usually inherited and triggered by some sort of shock or trauma. It is normally treated with insulin, which simply adds to the insulin produced by the pancreas. The old-age diabetes is usually caused by a breakdown of the pancreas as the result of eating too many sweets and carbohydrates, which the body turns into sugar. Old age diabetes is usually treated with pills. Before the age of 40, it is usually considered juvenile diabetes. After 40, it is usually considered old age diabetes. I was just north of 37. Which did I have?

The doctor recommended treatment using insulin injections, diet and exercise, as well as less stress. After a week in the hospital, my sugar levels were more or less in control, and I managed just that for the next 40-plus years, more or less in control.

Any diabetic who claims to have their sugar levels under control is probably lying. It is a constant struggle to maintain a balance with diet, exercise, medication and emotional stability. A diabetic vacillates between too high and euphoria and too low, approaching shock.

For me, it was a new challenge. One that demanded paying attention to what my body was telling me every minute of the day and night. While I was working, running conferences, attending meetings, making recommendations, I listened simultaneously to my inner condition, feeling the rise and fall of sugar in the blood, balancing emotional stress, exercise and diet. Once a day, I made sure to walk. I also walked between offices, up and down floors, to restaurants; whenever possible I walked. I avoided sugar, even though it was my favorite food, second only to fruits.

Up to then, I expected my body to do whatever I needed for it to do. I worked late and hard and I did not expect to have any rebellion from my body. There was no argument, it just better be there when I needed it for anything. I slept whenever there was time and ate whenever there was time. Now I needed to pay attention to daily rhythms, eat regular and proper meals, not because I felt like it, but because if I didn't my body would give me grief.

Just who was the boss? My body or me? At first I resented it. Why should I have to pay so much attention to what my body needed? Why couldn't it just make do with whatever scraps I happened to throw it? At first, I was even asked to weigh every bit of food I ate and count the calories. I tried, but you can guess that went by the board pretty soon. So I compromised; I was careful, but on the other hand I refused to be slave to my own body.

At least, I clearly distinguished between the needs of my body and the needs of Siegfried. I stayed the boss, and maybe that was a good thing. After all, the older one gets the less important the body becomes, and usually the more time it consumes. Staying in charge of it became a mighty lesson. "I'll agree to take some care of you if you in return continue to carry me about and supply me with the energy to get a few things done." The alliance was forged: The Treaty of Krefeld between Siegfried and his body.

29

Episode 20: Second Accident in Europe

I drove from Brussels to Krefeld, Germany. The roads were flat and uneventful. Here and there a village demanded that I slow down. Occasionally I passed a farm cart stacked high with hay, straw or manure, or once or twice the strange barrel-shaped carts with *Jauche* aboard to fertilize the fields. I was humming, glad to be on my way home for the weekend with the family.

The route required me to drive through a narrow strip of Holland. That meant customs and the usual delay, even though all European countries were on good terms and kept each other informed when necessary.

I pulled into the plaza in line behind a Mercedes and another Volkswagen. The Mercedes took a long time; they waved the Volkswagen through, and it was my turn. The customs officer took my passport and international drivers license and disappeared into the glass cubicle. I waited while they looked me up.

In the lane to the left of me, a lorry (truck) ground its gear into first and inched forward, belching smoke high into the air. As it moved forward, black exhaust sprayed from the tail pipe. I wondered how much of the greasy film sticks to the road and whether they had to wash it clean every now and then. I thought probably not, since the roadway was black with it for at least a hundred yards, all the way to the slight curve ahead.

Episode 20: Second Accident in Europe

The officer returned my papers and waved me through since I had nothing to declare and they believed me. I stepped on the gas and made it to 45 kilometers per hour as I approached the slight curve ahead. Suddenly, my windshield flooded in a brief shower; I turned on the wipers and slowly turned the wheel into the curve. Nothing happened as I turned the wheel. The car continued forward as if the wheel had nothing to do with its direction. I turned a little more and still nothing. The car continued in a straight line as the road slowly curved off to the right.

I glanced off the side of the first large tree and changed directions somewhat, but the second tree made me careen off across the road, through a fence, over a small hillock and suddenly everything was happening in slow motion. The car tipped to the right and agonizingly, slowly turned upside down, then right side up and then over again another time before coming to a stop.

At one point, my nose was right up against the floorboards, and I wondered how that could be, since the floorboards were so far down from the seat. I was conscious of glass shards and sparkling slivers cascading over me and out the side and back window holes. Mechanically, I turned off the key and unraveled myself from the steering wheel.

I opened the door with a little help from a young couple who had witnessed the accident and came rushing over on foot to help me. A police car pulled up on the road, and two officers came to assist me.

They took me to a doctor nearby, who announced that I was shaken up and bruised but miraculously uninjured as far as he could tell. The police told me my car was totaled and offered to have it towed away by a wrecking company. The police report would be sent to my insurance company. The doctor ordered a taxi for me and released me. I was only 35 minutes later than my expected arrival time at home in Krefeld, Germany.

"What happened to you?" my wife asked, eyeing my torn suit, oil spots on my shirt and tie and bruises along my right cheek.

"I had a little accident in Holland."

"What happened?"

I described the accident in great detail, but very slowly to match the slow motion of the experience. I lay down and reviewed the entire sequence again. I couldn't believe how vivid the details were burned into my consciousness. The slow turning of the car, my face touching the floorboards, how did that happen? I recalled the glass cascading over me and out the rear window, not a single sliver touching me. Every detail was vividly alive in my memory. What was going on with me?

Where was I while this accident was occurring? How is it that I was both the protagonist and the spectator simultaneously? Why was it all happening so slowly, almost deliberately, each segment of the experience a whole event in itself tied to the former segment and the later segment as though in time-lapse-sequenced photography? I was the subject and the photographer, but someone else was the stage manager. Was my Angel involved again? If so, how? Was she sheltering me in some way, or was she somehow instrumental in it, telling me something I should know?

Then I knew. While coming out of the customs check point, stepping on the gas, gathering speed, I was feeling buoyant, almost joyous, starting to hum a tune. My consciousness was lowered. I was not as alert as I usually am. I was partially in a dream, not fully awake. I was under the influence of my Angel.

The oil slick on the road from thousands of cars and trucks accelerating as they moved out of the customs check point was spread before me, a kind of killing field waiting for me. Then came the sudden downpour, only a cloudburst, but enough to make the road slick and unresponsive to my steering. Then that first tree straight ahead, but the bank at the side of the road tilting me slightly away so that it only slammed the side of the car. Crossing the road after the second tree turned me into it. Now I remember all the other cars had slowed down behind me to turn on windshield wipers, slowed down enough to get me across without ramming into them. The open field was suddenly soggy, the car turning over and over but stopping right side up.

What was I doing while all this was happening? Remember Siegfried, remember! I remember now. I was dying. Yes, now I know. I had given myself up. Sure that my life was over, not fighting it, but letting go of it. I was at peace and yet strangely expectant, waiting for my departure. I was realizing that somehow the life I had known and cherished was nearing a conclusion and that something else now had to happen. What? What happens after I die?

Well, here I was again. Did I die, or didn't I? What a strange matter it is to die and yet still be alive. I wondered whether there had been some mistake. Was I supposed to die, or not to die? Here I was again. I was alive. Not worse for wear it seems. While I lay there resting on my bed at home, I slowly adjusted to the idea that I was actually still alive and still available to do something worthwhile. Instead of it being the end, it suddenly felt like a beginning. I was given a second life.

This second life was different. It was qualitatively very different. My first life was one of exploration, finding myself. Every experience was full of joy and expectancy. It endowed me with an eagerness to discover. I woke up every morning determined to experience all there was to discover. My first life was all about me.

This second life was more like a sequel, having many of the same qualities, but now I was looking to serve. I wanted to devote all that I had become to serve other human beings and the Earth, our home in space. I was not interested so much in preservation or even eliminating pain, sorrow or sickness or even death. I was interested in what I can describe only as forward motion. I wanted to help all human beings move forward, develop further, become all they are endowed to become. I had placed all my confidence in the potential in every human being and in all humanity. It was stronger than hope. It was an all-abiding trust.

I wondered whether my Angel would co-inhabit this new biography of a second life just as she had participated so patiently in my first. Maybe even this second life would be more hers than mine. She still had to rely on me to live it and write it.

30

Episode 21: Third Accident in Europe

We had all been to the stable in Krefeld. Ruth and I watched our three children ride. They looked so professional with their riding coats, helmets and riding crops perched high on their horses. They went around and around, adjusting to different gaits and smiling proudly at us each time they passed.

We then bicycled home. The two boys and Ruth were in the lead on their own machines, but Angela, then aged 7, sat in a seat behind me on my bicycle. We were about one mile from home when a loud bang in front startled all of us, our bicycles wobbling slightly.

Angela leaned way out to see, because of course I obstructed her view of what was going on ahead. In so doing, we lost our balance, wobbled precariously against the curb and then crashed down onto the pavement. The others stopped and walked back to help us.

I felt fine and rose to my feet. Angela had already jumped up and was ready to climb aboard again. I couldn't stand on my right leg. It just hung there like a wet noodle. I had lost my connection entirely with that leg and none of my muscles worked.

We had to get home somehow. I dragged myself onto the bicycle seat and, using only the left leg, bicycled back home. Every now and then pain gripped me. I couldn't move or breathe. It was paralyzing. However, I knew that the pain was not the problem. Something else was wrong. I feared that a break had happened somewhere along the upper leg since I could not move any part of the lower leg, nor could I bend at the hip.

Arriving home, a friend came by and helped me to his car. Several times I came close to passing out, especially getting into the car seat. He put the seat way back so my leg did not need to bend very much. Somewhere on the drive to the hospital, I must have bitten through my lower lip.

Well, it was only a broken hip and the doctors were quite cheerful. It could be nailed together with a 6-inch-long, three-eighths-inch-thick nail. It meant it needed to be immobilized for about six to eight weeks and in a year the nail would be removed after everything had healed up nicely.

For once the doctors were absolutely correct, and their predictions were accurate. I learned that, when one breaks a bone, it is stronger where it heals than it was before. That is why we rarely break the same bone in the same place twice. Thank goodness for that.

It also meant I had to stay at home in Krefeld, while the office fended for itself with colleagues filling in and helping where and when they were needed. It made me wonder how much I was really needed.

From the time that I first broke my leg and it hung uselessly by my side, I found that I had gained a different relationship to the ground, at least that particular ground, the ground in Europe. For some reason my connection with Europe was severed. I had been born in Germany and still as a child my mother carried me along with my brother to the United States. I had my third birthday on Ellis Island, along with several million others escaping from the trouble brewing in Europe in 1935 and beyond. The thing is that I did not arrive in America on my own. I was carried in my mother's arms to this country.

Now I knew my time in Europe was over. I was no longer needed there, nor was my particular path through it to be continued. It took three accidents to finally get through to me. Now I felt the change. I felt a strong urge to return to the United States and wondered how I would manage that.

31

COMMENTARY ON ANGEL LOGIC AND DREAMS

From what I had experienced so far, logic does not seem to serve angels in the same way it does us. We use logic to get securely from one thought to the next. Some of us use linear logic, that is, we fix the second thought securely in our belief system and then see if we can get to it from where we are without jumping off into the unknown. In a sense we drag ourselves in a straight line to where we want to be. That is the architecture of all planning, strategic as well as tactical.

Others of us use what I call organic logic. We know where we are, and using our imaginative powers we evolve the next step organically out of our current position or condition. Men in general tend to favor linear logic, while women most often feel comfortable with organic logic. It is dangerous to form such generalities, but it cannot be helped if observation tends to support the generality, which is of course based on limited and highly skewed experience.

It seems angels can't figure out what we are doing with this funny logic of ours, whether it is linear or organic. Organic logic is a little closer to what they can experience, but still a mystery.

Angels apparently use what I call picturing logic. They are so organized that the reality confronts them in pictures, and their response to it is another picture closely related and meaningful in relationship to the first picture. However, the picture continuously evolves, never becomes static, and the truth of the picture is fully alive in it. Logic is not necessary to arrive at truth. Angel pictures are not snapshots. Each picture is the whole thing. Each picture contains all there is and never stops including what will be and was. Time beings don't cut and splice the way we do. Reality simply modifies all there is. They have the ultimate holistic perspective.

How do I know this? Any thinking and feeling person who investigates the various turning points in life and tries to penetrate into the evidence or footprints in their biography will notice that what intervenes has a different perspective. Our experience of life is sequential in time and moves from location to location while thinking. What intervenes is all-aware of past and future, blends them seamlessly and intervenes with tact and wisdom. I can't explain it more than that. I am counting on my readers opening their inner eyes to the mysteries in their own biography and discovering their angel's footprints in the turning points of their lives.

We tend to gnaw down to the bone when we analyze a problem or an event. The richness of it, the flesh and circulation in it, the beauty within it often eludes our analytical mode. We usually scratch away all the unessential, leaving only what is meaningless.

Our consciousness is not bad or flawed; it is just immature. We have a long way to go if we are to understand how an angel regards life. Perhaps our dreams come closer because we use an imaginative skill in our unconscious that transforms static conditions into stories. Falling out of bed can become a serious drama on a mountainous cliff. Becoming entangled in a pillow can become a struggle between life and death in a dream. Perspiring under a comforter can easily lead to a forest fire; even a fever can become a long dream.

32

Episode 22: The Golden Star Philosophy

My most vivid dreams seem to come when I am sick, feverish and somewhere between sleep and wide-awake consciousness. They like to take advantage of me when I am defenseless. This dream changed my life forever because it brought something really deep in my unconscious to the surface, an idea that could become an ideal.

I dreamt I was involved in a struggle of some kind. I did not know how I got into it. I was sure that it was a worthy cause. I felt called upon to defend something. An indistinct adversary gradually emerged quite clearly before me. Shocked to the core, I beheld the ugliest beast I had ever seen. Enormous claws jutted out into space-defending a hard-scaled body that stretched into infinity with every muscle clattering the scales as they bunched and scraped. The head of this beast resembled that of a dragon but it waffled between a sneer and a scowl. Every time it breathed a smoke-filled stench overcame me, followed by intense heat.

The smart thing would have been to run. Why are we never smart in our dreams? I felt called upon to battle a creature that was one hundred times my size. If I'd had a wondrous sword, I might have prevailed, as the legendary Nibelungen hero Siegfried eventually did. My mother named me after him, because she was sure the world needed a "warrior of light." I am afraid I hardly ever measured up to my own imagination of my namesake.

Instead, the creature grasped me in one claw, roared its triumph and belched fumes and heat in my direction. It was a long way from the earth to the beast's jaws. I struggled every inch of the way. The closer I was brought to the head, the hotter and more pungent the air became around me. It weakened me, despite the last semblance of courage I had mustered. High in the air and helpless, I finally gave up.

This was surely the end. I was powerless to do battle and helpless to protect myself. I realized I had reached the end of my strength, the end of my life. I let go and prepared myself to die as I hung in the air, dangling from a claw opposite the monstrous maw.

Through veiled eyes and clouded vision, I gazed for a last time at the horrible creature into whose power I had fallen. Something struck me as odd. I blinked. Looked again. Astounded, there on the forehead of this monster was a small shining gold spot. I blinked again and looked more closely. It was tiny, but there was no doubt it had the shape of a star. I gazed at it, full of wonder and surprise. How could it be that on something so ugly a beautiful golden star could grace its forehead? My whole mood changed, and I was filled with wonder.

In my dream, I became less and less aware of the creature. It seemed to melt away as I continued to look at this little star. The creature slowly disappeared in mists and shadows, leaving me unscathed and standing free.

When I awoke, I was wet from perspiration. The fever had broken and I began to mend. The doctor thought it amazing how quickly I recovered from a bad case of mumps at the age of 27. (Not a good time to have mumps.)

The fever and recovery was reflected in my dream. Something happening in my body gave the stimulus for a violent dream. A health condition became a long story, alive with color and drama. I was only half-conscious, yet remarkably imaginative. Just think what a drama my semiconsciousness had created out of a feverish condition. The so-called reality was the fever, and then what was the dream? It wasn't purely fantasy; there was some truth in it.

There was also something else in it; a kind of moral element shone through the story into my consciousness. Had I drawn a value from a still deeper consciousness? Did my unconscious, deep sleep instill a moral value into the dream from the other side? I began to wonder whether we are only alive in the whole universe when we are asleep, unconscious. Are we living with angels when we dream? Do we wake up subsequently to live with each other in what we experience as reality?

If the universe began with a big bang, it wasn't the whole truth. I suspected now that it began with a moral impulse, inspired an imaginative world, a kind of dream, and only recently solidified for our current perceptions. Perhaps humanity developed in this threefold way as well. If we began as a moral impulse, then dreamed our way into consciousness and now are waking to our responsibility to each other and the earth, I can better understand what is emerging in all of us as a social conscience. It is in our destiny right from the beginning.

The dream changed me. From then on in my life whenever confronted with obstacles, apparent enemies, painful circumstances or disagreements, I would look for the good and the beautiful. I knew that whatever one paid attention to tended to flourish, while what one ignored tended to fade, dissolve and lose its power. I found that focusing on something beautiful or good in the situation or person offered the best chance to find solutions and resolutions. From then on, I always looked for the good and the beautiful in everyone and everything. So far, I have always found it if I remembered to look for it. No matter how often I was confronted with something destructive, ugly or untruthful, if I remembered the lesson of my dream there always was something appealing, beautiful or truthful to be found. The golden star philosophy has guided the rest of my life.

A dream can extend its drama for apparent hours and yet scientists tell us it usually lasts only a few seconds. Time seems to be something elastic when we dream. A time being evidently experiences the values inherent in imaginative portrayal of reality. Logic that is flexible and pictorial has an impact in human consciousness. My Angel was alive in this dream.

SECTION SIX

HOME AT LAST

"Angel pictures are not snapshots. Each picture is the whole thing. Each picture contains all there is and never stops including what will be and was. Time beings don't cut and splice the way we do. Reality simply modifies all there is. They have the ultimate holistic perspective."

33

Episode 23: Coming Home

"I think we would like to see you back at headquarters. Find your replacement here, and you can certainly continue supervising him from New York...on a dotted-line basis, of course," my old boss on Park Avenue suggested somewhat firmly.

"That's all right," I said, hiding my joy very carefully. "If you think that best, I'll be glad to return."

"Now, I am sure you'll want to come over and look around to decide where to live, research some real estate and schools."

"No, Frank. I will move right into Spring Valley, New York. We know the people there and actually still have a house that we have subletted to friends these past two years. We can pack up and come whenever you are ready for me," I added cheerfully.

"Well, I am sure you'll want to research different schools and arrange for transportation and all the details involved in a move like this."

"No, Frank," I said, a bit puzzled by his insistence on a special trip to New York. "All of that I can arrange easily, since we'll be returning into a community we already know well."

"I imagine it could be a tremendous help to you to settle things in advance, and I am sure Ruth will be relieved to know you've done that. It could be scheduled for sometime in early December, and you could plan your move for the first week in January."

"I guess that could be helpful, and I can wind things up over here to suit that timing." I gave in, still not understanding, but knowing enough not to drive the exchange into the ground.

As it turned out, I met a number of the people I would be working with, including my own department staff. Several of those with whom I had lunch expressed their pleasure that I was returning to the top corporate job in executive development, offering to help and asking for help on several issues. It turned out to be a good move.

On January 1, our family arrived back in the United States. We were picked up at JFK International Airport, driven to Spring Valley, New York, and lodged temporarily in a guest house of the Threefold Educational Foundation and School.

It had all happened so quickly and so smoothly, this was my first chance to wonder what I was doing back here in the United States. I was absolutely certain that I had made the right decision, that I was in the right place, and yet had no idea why.

I started the daily commute from Spring Valley to Manhattan. After one or two tries by car that ended up taking nearly two hours each way, I then tried public transportation, which would mean taking a bus to the 42nd Street terminal and then a good walk to 50th Street and Park Avenue. Finally, I teamed up with a group of 8 other commuters into Manhattan, paying as a group to drive in a van, starting and stopping as needed to pick up fellow commuters and dropping them off at specific corners in Manhattan or at home. We took turns driving. Most of us slept on the trip except, of course, the one who had to drive.

I seemed to be the one who most often traveled either to another location in the United States or to Europe. Each of us paid by the month whether we used the van or not. That made it a stable situation and we all seemed to get along.

I rated a corner office with windows along two sides, furniture designed for comfortable small meetings and a secretary who was absolutely outstanding. She kept me out of a lot of trouble and made me look great.

One day, a corporate executive and friend stopped by my office. I knew he had a reason to see me, but he was having some trouble getting around to it. I waited patiently, knowing it would come out if it was important to him. Eventually it did!

"Sieg, do you have children?"

"Yes; 2 boys, a girl and 2 foster children, plus a number that seem to find their way into our house from time to time. How about you?"

"I have a son and 2 daughters. My son is 21 now. He took a year off before registering for college. He is now at Fairleigh Dickinson University."

"That's right here in New Jersey, isn't it?" It was just small talk, but I guessed whatever was on his mind had to do with that son.

"Yes. He's doing quite well. He seems very attracted to environmental studies and business ethics. We have many discussions... actually they seem mostly to be arguments."

"Arguments?"

"Yes. About both subjects! He has a lot of opinions about business and about ethics."

I was smart enough to keep quiet. Speaking sometimes draws people out, but often silence seems to work even better. I waited patiently, but he sat, still reluctant to go on.

"The next generation has its own ideas about what we should be doing. I've been lucky. Both my sons are creative, but they also seem to absorb what's good in my generation. Lucky me!" I finally ventured.

"I'm not so lucky. Richard doesn't approve of my working for ITT. He seems to have something against large multinational corporations. He thinks we are trying to gobble up the whole world, and that we don't care who gets hurt while we're doing it. From everything he has learned in college, he has decided that there is something ethically wrong about our existence and our business practices.

"He doesn't seem to mind the new convertible I bought for him, the fact that I pay for his tuition at Fairleigh Dickinson, or that he has a credit card on which he charges fairly significant amounts every month, for which I pay. He doesn't seem to put the two together—the advantages he receives and the work I do for ITT."

"Surely you can somehow bring that perspective home to him," I ventured.

"Oh, I try. I bring to his attention the catch-22 he's in, for which he has no answer. He seems to think that poverty is much more honorable than wealth and furthermore that he would respect me more if I did not do the work that feeds and clothes him. Maybe he's willing to live poorly in his mind, but I think in real life he would change his mind."

"That's an idea. Why not take away his credit card, hand him the bills from college and see if he likes being poor. Who knows, he might decide that living well is worth a little scaling down of his ideals."

"There's the rub. Even though I know he's not being fair to me and that he is wrong about my work, I don't have the heart to let him find out the hard way. Maybe he would quit college, get a job and end up supporting himself, perhaps meagerly but still adequately. I want him to have a good education and I want him to be as prepared as he can be to take a good paying job and to have a prosperous career much like mine."

"What does he want? How much does it matter what you want? I mean, in the end you can't shape him in your image."

"I know that; but at least he should have the possibility to chose my way if that's what he wants. Without a college education, he'll never get that chance."

We were interrupted in our conversation by the phone. His secretary wanted him for a meeting in his office in fifteen minutes, which was important for his career. He left me wondering whether the great gulfs between generations are ever resolved except by time and the ongoing progression of human progress.

The rest of the story I found out from him a few months later.

Harold Geneen, the president and CEO of ITT, was wrestling with a problem. It seemed that we were likely to lose a multimillion-dollar contract to build and operate a telephone switching system in Brazil, just west of Rio. While still thinking about what to do, he left his office on the 10th floor and moved toward the elevators. With him were the two other members of the office of the president.

He said, "We need someone to go down there and persuade the officials to see it our way, no matter what the cost."

Meanwhile, my friend arrived at the same elevators on the second floor, my floor, and when the elevator arrived he entered and meant to push the 7th floor button for his own office. By mistake, probably, he was still thinking about the issue with his son, and he pushed the wrong button, the one that would take him to the 10th floor.

"Damn!" he said, as this would make him late for his office meeting.

He arrived at the 10th floor just as Harold Geneen arrived at the elevators. The minute he saw my friend something clicked in his mind. He said, "You've spent a lot of time in Rio, as I recall. You organized the operational strategy for launching our telephone system and know all the officials, middle folks right up to the top."

"Yes, that's right," answered my friend.

"Meet me in my office in an hour. I think you can solve an important problem we have, don't you agree?" He turned to the other two members of the office of the president, and they both nodded their heads.

The rest I heard from my friend several months later. In order to obtain the contract for building, installing and operating a new telephone switching system in Brazil, my friend was authorized to spend up to one million dollars in a variety of payoffs, whatever it took to get the deal through.

Lest we misunderstand, it was customary in Brazil at the time that to obtain a contract for any work one had to tip all kinds of officials without any actual promise of success. The gifts had a way of gaining support. Sometimes a silent tipping war ensued, as each contender for a contract matched and exceeded other venders vying for the same job. No other approach seemed to work at that time. This was not an illegal practice there, but a "normal" way to obtain any large- or small-scale project contract.

When my friend told me about this new assignment he had received, he said, "Why did I push the wrong elevator button? If I had gone directly to my office on the 7th floor, I would not have run into Geneen and probably would not have landed this job. It was such an important job, a great opportunity for me. However, because of the arguments with my son, I began to question whether

I was actually doing something wrong. I know there was no other way to get business in Brazil, but so what. Maybe we should have insisted on a more straightforward approach. I did a beautiful job; we got the contract, and ITT is making a good profit, which more than covers the cost of doing business this way. However, I'm not sure we did the right thing. Furthermore, I am hesitant to tell my son or my wife or any of my friends about it. That's a sure sign that I prefer not to take any credit except in the small circle of people at ITT who know what I did and appreciate me for doing it. I also wonder whether any of them would come to my defense if, for some reason, I was challenged and had to go public."

"You know," I said to my friend, "this issue seems to have been lurking in your life for some time and has just now surfaced into the daylight. Maybe it is something you have to face and deal with. Maybe tell your son about it and tell him about your doubts, as well? Maybe he's more on your side than you give him credit for."

"That's a thought," he said.

I have not seen him since that last conversation. He remained heavily involved in the project in Brazil, and may still be there for all I know.

This little episode fascinated me. Why was it that he pushed the wrong button? Or was it the right button on a deeper level? How is it that his arguments with his son started some internal unease that perhaps engineered the occurrences around the elevator? The sequence of the argument with his son, the conversation with me, the events around the elevator on the 10th floor, and his agreement to take on the assignment is too neat to be brushed off as accidental. There is a kind of angelic logic in it that surpasses our conscious decision-making.

Seeing the footprints of an angel in someone else's biography is rare, unless all the details are disclosed. It seems the devil is in the details, but so is the angel. Most historians do not bother with the very fine details that reveal the intervening of an invisible being. The chain of little events and small decisions, even the accidental details, are much more revealing than are the big decisions, large meetings and conferences, though they are often the result of some smaller sequence of events.

Although the angel cannot move around furniture or arrange meetings, it seems powerful in exerting influence on the thought and feeling life of those who do the arranging, or at least the deciding. Of course, we do not know what else is going on behind the scenes. Nor do we know the agendas of such beings and what influences them. Now that would be a historical research project, indeed—to show how a huge number of incidental events preceded a major event, revealing the influences stemming from the real causes that make use of the individuals who acted in space on their behalf. What would that tell us about the start and ending of world wars? Would we discover how some events are mirror images of an invisible sequence of events unknown to us and entirely behind the scenes?

Isn't it possible that the world wars were actually mirror images of struggles between angelic beings, and then were fought and reflected in our so-called historical events? Could it be that we are the special shadows of beings struggling with the outcome of our evolution? I think in my next life, I will be a historian trying to get at the real causes of our intermingled biographies called history.

34

Episode 24: The Big Three Visit

While employed at ITT In 1975, I agreed to serve as treasurer of the Anthroposophical Society in America. It was a pro bono job in addition to my job at ITT. At the same time, I also took on the presidency of the Threefold Educational Foundation and School. It all was part of my search for the real reason I had returned to the U.S. All three jobs demanded a great deal of my time and energy.

As treasurer of the Anthroposophical Society, I was often subjected to the demands and challenges of the members. One of them was particularly insistent. I will call him Norman in honor of the many fond memories he afforded me.

"I don't understand why you don't get in touch with them and get them over into this country."

"Who?"

"Ernst Barkoff, that's who. I've been telling you about him for months. He is the attorney in Bochum, Germany, and founded the Gemeinschafts Bank, which has a whole different approach to lending."

"Oh yes, I remember now," I admitted somewhat wearily. Norman had accosted me on numerous occasions and urged me to get in touch with this interesting German banker. He thought the members would be interested in hearing about what he was doing.

"Remind me again, Norman, " I responded almost by rote. "How could he be of help to us?"

"He has discovered a way to finance biodynamic farms in Germany. He gathers the customers of such a farm, lends them each a sum, let's say 2,000 Deutsche Marks, but instead of giving the money to the customer, he gives it to the farm as operating money for one year. The farm's 200 customers each borrow 2,000 DM, giving the farm 400,000 DM for its operating budget. Each customer pays off the bank loan in twelve months. This process serves to get 200 people interested and involved in supporting a farm. I think they also occasionally work on the farm at key production peaks and probably get some of the products free of charge. I don't know all the details, but there is a lot of excitement in Germany about this approach. It's a little like our CSA, but having a bank involved introduces additional benefits for the customers as well as for the farmers. You should get them over here to talk about their approach."

"I'll think about it, Norman, and talk with the Executive Committee and then get back to you," I answered, wondering a little about my workload and whether I could fit anything else into it, and about the meager budget of the Anthroposophical Society.

At the next meeting of the Executive Meeting, Henry Barnes, the chair, opened up a new topic.

"I wonder whether we shouldn't ask Ernst Barkoff to tour this country, giving lectures at some of the key locations where members could hear about his work."

"Norman has been after me for some time to get him over here," I volunteered.

"I have just received this letter from the treasurer of the Anthroposophical Society in Switzerland, offering to support his coming over for ten days, along with Rolf Kerler and herself. We should get out the word and see how many of our branches and groups would like to host them on their tour."

"They should start in Spring Valley and New York City, then let's see who else is interested," I suggested.

"What about the budget? Can we afford it? The Europeans have offered to help pay for the tour, but have not mentioned any particular sum. I also think the Bochum Bank will offer some support as part of their public relations budget. I guess they might get more depositors from the membership this way," Henry mused.

"I will work on the finances, if you do the actual arranging. Based on roughly seven stops, starting in New York and ending in California, I'll put together a budget for the trip and figure out how to pay for it."

I understand the Bochum Bank will pay for all the airline tickets if we handle all actual transportation, room and board," Henry added.

"That's a big help, because we will ask each location to handle all the local expenses. They can charge entrance fees to the lectures and provide potluck meals and nice rooms in private homes for each of them."

"Well, it's settled then. I will formalize the invitation, get in touch with each of the main centers in this country and schedule the visits at each. I think we can assume that they can arrive in Spring Valley, stay at the main house of the Threefold Educational Foundation and School and have the first lecture in their auditorium," concluded Henry.

In June 1977, Ernst Barkoff, Gisela Reuter and Rolf Kerler arrived at JFK Airport and were driven directly to the Threefold Educational Foundation and School. Charlotte Parker, the patroness of the foundation insisted on housing them in her private home, which was seen as a great honor.

I greeted them in careful anticipation. Ernst Barkoff was a tall, impressive man with friendly eyes and a gravelly voice. He greeted me in German. We chatted a bit more in German and eventually I found out that he did not speak English. That was a shock. None of us ever thought of this eventuality. How egocentric of us. We just assumed that everyone spoke English, never dreaming or preparing for the possibility that our main speaker at seven locations throughout the U.S. would lecture in German.

"Well, you will translate for me, no?" Ernst smiled, a twinkle in his eyes.

Now, I was very good at getting out of things like this. One time at ITT, I wiggled myself out of having to implement a program I didn't like. It seemed that Harold Geneen thought every executive at ITT should be a kind of ambassador for ITT in his or her local town. He first voiced this idea at a meeting in the large oval conference room at ITT headquarters.

"I'd like you, Sig, to put together a training program that would make every one of our executives a good and effective spokesperson for ITT culture and the benefits to every community of having ITT represented. Can you do that?" he asked.

At ITT, it was not politically correct to reject an idea, any idea, but especially not an idea of the president and CEO. I glanced around the room and saw the warning looks on the faces of the executives I knew, who were part of my internal network.

"Yes, I think that can be done, Hal, but I wonder what they will say. Shouldn't Ned Gerrity craft the speech from a PR perspective first? Then I will work on the design of the program itself," I volunteered.

"That's a good idea, Ned; what do you think?"

In shock, Ned reworked his facial expression and cleared his throat. "I can do that, Hal, but that's just a detail. The full design of the program with some of the points highlighted should be worked out as part of the development of all executives of ITT. I'm sure I can come up with the speaking points as soon as I have some idea of the programmatic design." He'd managed to sidestep gently.

"Okay; then it's settled. Ned, you work on the message, and Sig will work your message into a program for all ITT executives," he concluded.

The eyes of all my friends in the room registered relief and smiled approval at me. Chances were the message would get tied up in approval processes and eventually get farmed out to a consultant and gradually disappear in the bureaucracy of the corporation.

So, I had lots of training on how to get out of implementing someone else's bright ideas. I knew how to avoid doing something I didn't want to do.

When Barkoff asked me to translate for him, I blanched. My mother often spoke to me in German all through my early childhood. I even took German as my language in college. I understood quite a bit of German, but had only a feeling for words, not the actual English translation.

I answered, "Yes." I couldn't believe I did it; I said yes.

To this day, I marvel at my audacity and foolishness.

The next evening, I waited by the side of Ernst Barkoff in the Threefold Educational Auditorium. We waited for the introduction to finish and then, accompanied by the usual expectant applause, we both climbed onto the stage and stood facing the audience. Every seat in the auditorium (about 210) was occupied, and the side aisles, as well as the rear standing section, were completely filled.

Ernst Barkoff began to speak. After almost a minute, he was still speaking. I did not understand every word, but I could tell he was eloquent and masterful in forming his ideas and feelings. He spoke about money and its connection to human consciousness.

After the first minute, he continued without looking at me.

I was overwhelmed. I think I understood most of it, but the ideas were so lofty, so complicated and so inspiring. The audience was spellbound, since nearly half of them understood German, and because his charisma charmed everyone.

I was paralyzed because I was in deep trouble. I thought, maybe I should ask to be excused, and we could find someone else. I was too numb even to do that. Besides, my reputation in this community would be soiled forever.

A very strange event then occurred. I hadn't planned it. It happened almost of its own accord. Perhaps the waves of fear had something to do with it.

I regressed. I became a small child, perhaps around three years in age. I listened, my mouth partly open. I was all ears. I had no defenses, no filters, no subjective reactions. I took it all in exactly as it poured out of Ernst Barkoff.

After about 4 minutes of astounding rhetoric, he paused and then turned to me and gestured for me to translate. I was not capable of an accurate translation since I had not taken a single note.

Instead I began to speak in English and imitated what was now living in me as the result of his speaking. I simply let out in English what I had experienced in German. It resounded in the hall. Nobody laughed. Nobody objected. Nobody demanded my resignation. It seemed to be all right.

An hour and 15 minutes later, he drew his lecture to a close with a tremendous vision of what could happen in the future, then bowed his head. After the translation, the applause was thunderous, and he turned to me smiling. Quietly, he said, "You really understood me and did in English what I did in German." It was the highest compliment I had ever received.

I translated for him at two other locations. Then, at the conclusion of his tour, we were in the car on the way to the airport, along with John Alexandra, when he turned toward us from the passenger seat in the front and asked, "When will you start something in America like our bank? America needs a whole new banking approach. The old ways are dying and in decline. They will go on still for a while, but the life is no longer in them. Something totally new is wanted."

We were stunned and had no idea what to say. It was a new idea, and both of us wanted to respond in some way, but we were silent.

He continued, "I feel we are colleagues. When you start, let us know what you need and we will help you. Colleagues in this work stand by each other through thick and thin."

Although this conversation took place in German, we understood what he was asking.

All three of these wonderful people left for their homes in Bochum, Germany, and John and I began to meet once a week early in the morning at Hamburger Heaven down in the Manhattan financial district.

35

Episode 25: Birth of RSF Social Finance

John Alexandra and I began to meet for breakfast once a week in a basement restaurant in the financial district of downtown New York City. The restaurant was called Hamburger Heaven. I'm not sure what to say about the appropriateness of the name, but it served us well.

We began to struggle with what we saw as the need to bring greater understanding and new spiritual impulses into the movement of money. We also saw the difficulties and realized that dealing with money was a little bit like trying to pick a rose out of a thorn bush. Nevertheless, our basic concepts were ironed out in Hamburger Heaven early in the morning before the business day opened on Wall Street, and the hordes of financially astute humans poured out of the subways and through the streets to disappear into the skyscrapers of downtown New York City.

We met sometimes at our homes in the evening, struggling to understand the nature of money. Mark Finser was drawn into the project in an interesting way. He had been visiting in Indiana when he needed an operation and rushed back to a hospital near our home, where he discovered that his employer had absconded with the health insurance money, leaving him without coverage. This led him, quite independently, to become concerned about money and health insurance and interested in changing the manner in which employees and employers interact over such issues as money and health insurance.

Mark's job required supervising a number of social workers and attendants in a community for emotionally challenged teens. He was a good manager and adept at involving others around issues.

That is how he happened to be in our home recovering from his operation while these discussions were taking place. He connected his own concerns over money with the entity that appeared to be forming. As a volunteer, he started to get involved with the ideas of RSF, took a definite interest, and became part of the founding group. Eventually he came along on our first site visit with a potential client and was hooked. Now there were three of us, John, Mark and myself.

We explored putting some ideas onto paper in a kind of crude brochure. John Alexandra was using a word processor on a computer in the office of the Threefold Educational Foundation. He threw away, into the wastebasket, the first version of the brochure and worked on another.

Ann Stahl, a kindergarten teacher at Green Meadow Waldorf School, was very interested in recycling paper whenever she could. In passing the wastepaper basket near John, she picked out the discarded first draft of the RSF brochure, looked at it, and asked John what it was. That's how Ann became involved.

I describe this level of detail to show how the choreography played out, how the key people were drawn in through a variety of accidental events and coincidences—Mark through the fact that he happened to be recovering from his operation in the house where RSF was shaping itself, and Ann by happening to be in the office where the brochure was being created, happening to look into the wastebasket and happening to see John there and asking, "What's this?" Now there were four of us.

One evening in Harlemville, New York, I attended a concert given by a very talented woman playing Chopin. She played wonderfully and was very much appreciated. That evening, I was introduced to the pianist's husband, Philip Mees. Strange, isn't it, that he happened to be a banker, a VP at Manufacturers Hanover Trust? Philip had been in a study group for years discussing Rudolf Steiner's ideas on the world's economy and money. He had become frustrated because the study did not lead to practical applications of some sort. When he heard about the beginnings of RSF, he felt that this was a chance to bring Steiner's ideas into practice.

Accidental, unplanned occurrences like that were happening right and left. We talked, and it was clear that our founding group was forming itself out of the intricate choreography of the world that inevitably brings together the right people for important initiatives. There were now five of us.

The five of us began meeting for a year at various places as needed, sometimes in one of our business offices and many times over the phone. We were hammering out the basic intentions. We wanted clarity in how to proceed and were searching for the right language to express these intentions. Very soon, it became clear that the ultimate purpose was to change how the world views money and to change how we work with money. For all of its obvious characteristics, the real identity and potential for the future of money seemed illusive.

All kinds of hypotheses abound on how to make money, how to spend it judiciously to get the best deal, and how to put it to work. Nobody that we knew around us was considering the effects of our many monetary transactions on our culture. Pessimists abounded, but where were the optimists for the future of money? Who was championing a new approach to its movement and social effects?

The founding group at RSF struggled with texts of Rudolf Steiner's lectures, *World Economy*, with many questions: What is capital, really? When did it arise in history, and why is it burgeoning in our economy? What is interest, and how should we all work with it? What is the role of money in human society, and why are we not satisfied with its current, apparent power? We gradually concluded that we wanted to work primarily with the transactions of borrowing/lending and with giving/receiving. Buying/selling didn't seem to be where we could be the most useful at the time. We began to form our purposes as we studied. It soon became obvious that studying money had to go side by side with doing something practical that involved money. Every concept we explored cried out for a practical application. We needed a client who was doing something worthwhile and needed money. It was as simple as that. We yearned to demonstrate our ideals in practice.

John Alexandra began working on the internal accounting system, to make it transaction based on and sensitive to the transactional nuances we intended to incorporate into the client statements and reports. We wanted our future clients to be able to see what their money was doing in the world when reading their statements. Ann Stahl began by assisting John and preparing and operating a small office in John's garage in Spring Valley, New York. Mark and I began focusing on sources of funding and potential clients. We used a small room in my home in Chatham, New York. Our job was to become the face of the enterprise, while John and Ann worked on the internal structures to sustain and make any work of RSF practical and secure.

The founding group decided to adopt the incorporated structure of the Rudolf Steiner Foundation and transform it into an active social instrument. There remained $6,000 in the checking account of RSF, which would soon be donated to a cancer research clinic in Switzerland. We knew this amount would soon be gone and we would have a zero balance in the RSF bank account.

In late 1983, the Pine Hill Waldorf School in Wilton, New Hampshire, burned to the ground, leaving some 120 children and a dozen teachers without a home. The first tangible assignment of RSF was to work with this homeless school. The two founders and leading teachers of the school were karmically connected with me. One, Ann Courtney Pratt, was my classmate at High Mowing School. The other, Daniela Patrick Rettig, participated with me in a study group in New York City and was a dear friend. You may remember she joined with Ruth and I at Camp Glen Brook to create the little operetta, "Ocean Born Mary." The call for help from the school was a call out of deep karmic connections reaching into the distant past and could not be ignored. Moreover, the founders of RSF were eager to take on a project and welcomed this challenge with enthusiasm.

The RSF volunteers piled into a car and traveled to New Hampshire. It was exciting to have a first opportunity to fumble with the words that conveyed the RSF mission and purpose. We met with the teachers, an architect who had returned from England, also to answer the call, and many of the parents. In the face of this tragedy, we were astounded by the forward-looking determination of those people. They undoubtedly wanted to rebuild and continue as a school.

Every person who spoke with us was able to describe in vivid pictures what kind of facility they longed to build. Even the children had drawn pictures of their wishes for a school. The architect summarized the elements as (1) connectivity to nature, (2) filled with light and open space, and (3) humanly proportioned and not box-like. He then began putting the school community's dreams into architectural drawings.

RSF participated in an all-school meeting in which many expressed their enthusiasm and determination to rebuild and flourish. High Mowing School, the sister school in the same town, offered forty-five acres of its land across the road from its campus. High Mowing felt that particular parcel of land would not be needed by them and welcomed Pine Hill Waldorf School to become a close neighbor with common philosophical, ideological and educational approaches. All of these fortuitous happenings boded well for the future. One of the teachers, Arthur Auer, who was on sabbatical leave, agreed to spearhead the project along with active trustees of the school. RSF volunteers acquired a growing confidence in the people and the project.

Life sometimes gives us very little chance to get ready for the challenges that face us. At the time the RSF volunteers plunged naively into these unknown responsibilities out of sheer love and enthusiasm. Challenges bring out of people what is necessary to deal with the challenges. No one would ever grow if not faced with the unasked-for challenges of life. The world of necessity, what we are challenged with, makes us creative and brings out the hidden talents and purposes that lie deep in our souls. *We become free in how we respond.* The world of necessity comes at us from without as though it is not part of us, but the moment we are so confronted we have extraordinary freedom in how we respond. It is possible that whatever freedom we have is a gift from the necessities with which we are forced to deal.

The RSF volunteers returned to New York after a second visit. We pondered what had been done. We had promised to help with a loan of $500,000! We wondered how we were going to do that. The

$6,000 had been sent to the cancer research clinic in Switzerland and there was no money in the RSF bank account.

The fact that all of us fell in love with Pine Hill Waldorf School turned out to be an important lesson and provided us with a significant operating procedure. It was realized that every time any of us advised or visited a project, a wonderful process of seduction would be put into motion. We realized that leading with the heart had a natural consequence of falling in love with the wonderful people in the project and would lead to an intense desire to help.

It was decided that, whenever possible, no one from RSF would go alone to visit a project. There would always be a second person along to supplement and adjust the process as it evolved. Moreover, RSF would need a process back in the home office that was called "cold" to offset the impact of the "warm" site visit. It was reasoned that falling in love with the client was inevitable and RSF needed to institutionalize the counter balance in order to maintain objectivity and balance. These decisions contributed greatly to the ultimate success of RSF.

RSF began with a project in need, a life situation that required money to flow, to move. *This wonderful work did not begin with the acquisition of money but with the recognition of a need and by facilitating the movement of money in the service of life.* The project and its need seemed to pull in the investors and that began the special RSF way of working with money. RSF as the lender had to make visible the need for funds to support the rebuilding project of the Pine Hill Waldorf School. Thus RSF found it necessary to ask for support, not for itself, but for a worthwhile project. RSF was only the reliable intermediary to facilitate the movement of money from where it was less needed to where it was more needed. Relationships matter immensely and always will.

Dominic DiSalvo was serving on the board of trustees at Pine Hill Waldorf School. All the loan details were negotiated with him in particular. He earned our respect. His straightforward intelligence, creativity and vision impressed us all. In this way, RSF gradually enlisted the sixth member of the founding group. His wonderful spatial and social imagination solved many a problem and guided us from a position of strength and integrity.

Mary Theodora Richards, an elderly woman and a friend of my family, whom we had chosen to care for in our home, heard all the conversations regarding the Pine Hill Waldorf School's situation. She had experienced the formation and creation of a mission for RSF. She now responded out of her immense desire to help and made the first "investment" in RSF.

It is interesting to note the karmic circumstances surrounding the meeting with Theodora Richards, as she liked to be called. Many years earlier, I had the opportunity to operate a biodynamic food co-op out of our apartment in New York City. People interested in such food placed their orders every week. A truck would deliver the food in bulk.

I remember filling the elevator several times while other tenants in the building waited patiently, and eventually not so patiently. To our surprise, our co-op grew dramatically. Within a matter of weeks we had to fill as many as 78 orders. One day when the truck delivered, we had to make 5 or more trips in the elevator. Then my wife and I broke the bulk amounts into each order, did the billing, and by late afternoon people began arriving to pay for and pick up their orders. The superintendent of the building warned us that we couldn't go on doing our business out of a residential apartment. Down the street from us was a vacant little store measuring 20 by 15 feet. We decided to rent it and operate the co-op from the store once a week.

The business grew and we were forced to open it on a second day, and eventually had it open 5 days a week and began to make deliveries ourselves to people's apartments all over Manhattan, as well as other boroughs and even New Jersey along the Hudson River.

One day, a station wagon arrived at the store, delivering a dozen biodynamic lettuce heads, each wrapped in tissue paper. It was obvious that they had been harvested that morning and were as precious as gold. They had come from a farm in Chester, New York, run by two women, Marjorie Spock and Theodora Richards. Both were very active in the biodynamic–organic movement and had done a great deal of research on the harmful effects of pesticides and artificial fertilizers. They were among the first biodynamic farmers in America and provided their research to Rachel Carson for her book *The Silent Spring*.

Our store became so popular that we met with several suppliers and considered the idea of opening a biodynamic supermarket. Two of the suppliers offered to form a partnership with me. We each would capitalize the market with $5,000, which would give us a total of $15,000 to start. That would cover the rent, utilities, and other expenses for up to three months. I traveled to the farm of Marjorie Spock and Theodora Richards and described the project to them. Theodora was excited about opening the first biodynamic supermarket in New York City, and when I left I had a check in my pocket for $5,000, a personal gift to me to cover my share of the partnership.

During the following weeks, the partners met several times. Each time, new wrinkles developed in our relationship. At one point, it began to look like my $5,000 was going to be the only cash invested; the other partners would put up services and goods of one kind or another. I became uneasy and consulted a friend who was very blunt; he advised, "If there is the slightest mistrust, don't do it!" I eventually decided not to go ahead with the idea. It was still a good idea, but the risks seemed too one-sided. I also was not a hundred-percent sure that my career path was to be a grocer. I informed the other two that I was backing out. There was great disappointment all around, and we parted ways. Karma apparently has an infinite number of sides and nuances to it.

I returned the check for $5,000 to Theodora Richards and earned the dubious honor of being the first person ever to return a gift to her. We became good friends, and when she needed a place and people to care for her many years later, we offered our home in Chatham, New York. That is the story of how Theodora Richards came to live in our home and take an interest in the creation of RSF. The founders of RSF had conceived the idea of transforming the Foundation into a vehicle for investors and borrowers to become conscious of one another and together make money move in socially constructive ways.

We imagined many people desiring social change investing in RSF and being informed of worthwhile projects, which their funds were making possible. Theodora Richards became the first investor in RSF. She was thrilled with the idea that she could help RSF do its work, while simultaneously helping the Pine Hill Waldorf School. She also marveled at the idea that lending could become charitable as well as giving.

We found that by speaking everywhere on behalf of the Pine Hill Waldorf School, other people began to lend RSF their savings to use in funding such a worthwhile project. Without any money of its own and without any credit, using the money invested in RSF by socially conscious human beings in turn enabled the RSF to lend $500,000 to the Pine Hill Waldorf School.

Recently at a ceremony that celebrated the successful history and current accomplishments of the Pine Hill Waldorf School special thanks were given to RSF, which bridged the crisis faced by the school and helped them to move into their beautiful new facilities.

At the same time, I was also able to thank the Pine Hill Waldorf School and give it credit for launching RSF toward its remarkable growth and service. How fruitful work can be when karma among the people is healthy and leads to collaborative work. I began to base most of my judgments, business, as well as personal, on a sensing of the karmic connections revealed in action.

Today, more than 25 years later, more than 1,000 individuals and organizations have invested more than $120 million in RSF in carefully managed investment funds so that worthwhile projects could be financed successfully. During those more than twenty-five years, almost $160 million has been loaned out doing good work in society. The results are visible all over the United States and in other countries as well. The loans are of course repaid over time, so the $160 million was turned over several times. That's the wonderful side effect of such an investment. It is like getting triple or quadruple social mileage out of the same funds.

From its position as intermediary, RSF could observe the movement of money enveloped by the ideals and values of the investors, as it brought about socially constructive projects. Deficits have been overcome and financial health restored, and auditoriums, gymnasiums, arts buildings, classrooms, and many other projects have been accomplished, many times by non-profit organizations the banks were afraid to finance.

For a more detailed description of the financial innovations and approaches of RSF Social Finance, read *Money Can Heal*, published by SteinerBooks.

36

COMMENTARY ABOUT ANGEL CHOREOGRAPHY

What is the difference between a huge snarl of different colored string and a tapestry? They both involve different colors, string, knots and interweaving. They both take time to develop and both are the tangible consequence of a number of movements and actions. Of course, the tapestry gives us pleasure while the snarl of string gives us grief.

The only difference between the two is that one comes about accidentally while the other is planned and executed according to plan. The design of a tapestry stands behind its execution. The design was there first, is active throughout its creation and is fulfilled by intentional activity. The design remains invisible but is fulfilled in the final product.

The snarl of string reveals its lack of design. It is chaotic and comes about through a sequence of accidental, unplanned movements or actions.

Is a human life, a single biography, more like a snarl of string or more like a tapestry? Thornton Wilder in his little book *The Bridge of San Luis Rey* attempted to query whether there was any design in the fact that five specific people were on the bridge when it collapsed. He explored all five biographies, described them in detail, and left the question somewhat unanswered. My college professor claimed that Wilder was making it clear that there was no design that brought those five people together.

I insisted that each life moved inexorably toward the event on the bridge and that the design was artistic, not discernibly rational.

To uncover the design we needed to use imagination and feeling rather than intellect alone. As you can imagine, the argument was never resolved except to demonstrate two different perspectives not necessarily mutually exclusive but nevertheless leading to a different conclusion. My secret conclusion was that the professor lacked courage to gainsay his own intellect.

A lifetime of experience and collaborative working with my Angel has taught me that the design behind my biography is alive in the living of it and is essentially artistic in its nature. Because it is a design of life, there are remarkable differences from the design of a tapestry. The design must make allowances for interventions and unexpected occurrences. A lifetime is more a work of art than the consequence of natural law. The intertwining of activity and material is creative rather than purely scientific. Any purview of a lifetime requires not only the science of the visible but also the science of the invisible.

In a dance performance the dancers, the costumes, the music and the stage sets are all very important. We notice their importance because these are all factors that we are able to see and hear. They signify their existence by appearing to our senses and we believe what we see and hear and do not bother to analyze the sound waves and speed of light. We can devote ourselves to enjoying them.

What is not seen is probably more contributory to our pleasure than we know. The management of stagehands, the organization of scene changes and the tremendous amount of practicing that goes into every performance are assumed but not seen. The efforts of writers and composers are also unseen. All such work is behind the scene; it has gone into what is seen and now lives in the visible, but is in itself invisible. That is the nature of all visible creativity of human beings, whether in shaping a machine, a painting, a musical composition or a dance performance. Creativity remains invisible while its results become visible.

In a dance performance, the work of the choreographer is truly invisible. We don't even see the result. The forms, positioning and relationships brought about by the choreography go almost unnoticed. The choreography speaks to us in the movements, colors and sounds, but remains invisible.

Just as choreography is among the highest invisible creations of the human being, so is it the stuff of angel activity. Every time we look at our lives and attempt to glimpse the choreography in it, we look directly into angel creativity. We are developing the ability to see the invisible, sometimes called clairvoyance.

When I look at the events and coincidences around the birth of RSF Social Finance, described so elaborately above, I try to fathom the choreography buried in the happenings. The whole picture of my life becomes meaningful as it intertwines with other lives.

Below I present the same occurrences that happened with the query of "suppose it had not happened?" Then I am closer to observing the choreography.

1. Suppose I had not gone to Europe in 1970. Would I still have discovered my real connection with America? Without my three revealing accidents in Europe, would I have returned to the U.S. with such openness to what would next challenge me? Suppose I had not returned to the U.S. just at that time would I have become involved as the treasurer of the Anthroposophical Society in America, especially since my teacher in grade school was chairman of the council? If I had not been in Europe for two years, not the treasurer of the Society and not connected to Norman, would I have been in a position to invite the three bankers from Bochum to give their talks on a tour of the U.S.? If I had not met Barkoff in Germany, had not experienced the events in ITT around power and service, would I have had the impulse to say "yes" when he asked me to translate for him? Furthermore, would I have said "yes" to translating for Barkoff, and would I have discovered the hidden talent of reverting to my childhood if in my early years I had not gone to the Waldorf school, where childhood

is honored and revered? Suppose John Alexandra and I had not been in the car together returning Barkoff to the airport. Would we have jointly felt compelled to "do something"? Suppose none of the above had happened. Would RSF Social Finance exist today?

2. Suppose Mark Finser had not been drawn to Indiana to visit a girlfriend, would he have fallen ill and needed an operation? Why did he come home for the operation and recuperate in our home? There were perfectly good hospitals in Indiana and it would have spared him the trip while sick and in pain. What if he had not returned home for the operation and experienced the beginnings of RSF? Would he have been drawn into the field of money if his employer had not absconded with the health insurance money that also ended his employment? He had risen so rapidly in his employment that in a very short time he managed nearly 400 people engaged in the social/service field. Without this experience would he have been ready to manage the intricate transactions of RSF? If his employment had not ended in this way, would he still be in the same organization today, doing valuable work, but not available for RSF?

3. Meanwhile, if Ann had not been needed in the Kindergarten at the Green Meadow Waldorf School, would she still have discovered the fundamental connection between spirit and matter necessary for RSF to exist? What if she had not taken on the small but important task of making sure paper got recycled at the school, would she have accidentally found the first draft of the RSF brochure? If she had not found the first draft of the RSF brochure, would she have asked John about it and been drawn into the circle forming around the birth of RSF? Would she have volunteered to help if her whole life sequence had not prepared her for this new but exciting opportunity? Would she have developed such outstanding advisory and consulting skills?

4. Meanwhile, had Philip Mees not been studying the economic lectures of Rudolf Steiner in a group that met in New York City, would he still have longed to apply them in some practical way to life? Suppose his wife had not been asked to play Chopin in Harlemville, New York, where I lived, would we have ever met? If Manufacturers Hanover Trust had not decided to offer early retirement to Philip, would he have been available to do so much for the forming of RSF, not just the many meetings and planning, but also eventually the employment with RSF? What about joining Mark and Ann as the first somewhat-compensated employees of the organization? Would he have been able and willing to help form RSF without all the early preparation and events in his life?

5. Meanwhile, suppose Dominic and Cindy DeSalvo had not become interested in Waldorf education, would they have moved to Wilton, New Hampshire, for the sake of their children? Would they have wanted their summer residence to become their home all year round without the presence of the Pine Hill Waldorf School? If they had not gotten deeply involved in a series of workshops and classes that helped parents of the school understand and experience the unique curriculum of the Waldorf school, would Will Sullivan have asked Cindy, and then later Dominic, to join the Board of Trustees for the school? If Dominic had not been on the Board just as the school burned down, would he have been involved in the relationship with RSF and would we have recognized in him the outstanding, highly active trustee that he was? If these events had not occurred and coincided exactly with the founding of RSF, would it exist today?

6. What if I had not gone to high school with Ann Pratt and studied Rudolf Steiner with Daniele Rettig and others, would they have appealed to RSF when their school, which they founded, was destroyed by fire?

7. Meanwhile, if I had not said "yes" to translating for Barkoff, would I have ended up with the treasure of insight and inspiration in me needed for the founding of RSF Social Finance?

Suppose all these happenstances were not in the several biographies of the early founders. Would RSF exist today? All these coincidences, leading up to the right people being at the right places in their lives, coming together under the right circumstances ready to take initiative, are difficult to accept as purely accidental. The time was right for RSF to be born and the midwives assembled to see it through.

Even going back in all the lives of the original founders of RSF it is possible to discern the beginnings of this ingenious choreography. Every event in each of the biographies contributed in various degrees as preparation for the founding of RSF. One could maybe ask, "Was RSF already working behind the scenes, engaging the angels of each founder, collaborating to prepare them all to be in the right place at the right time?" Did we give birth to RSF or did RSF arrange all the events leading to the incarnation of its organization, its body on the earth? Did each of us before we were born accept the task to be ready for RSF when the time was right?

We all had to be willing to accept the challenge when it presented itself to our consciousness. We all had to bring something unconscious to the surface in order to manifest RSF in space. Angels had to be working in the stream of time, aware of past and future flowing together into living biographies that culminated in 1984 at the founding of RSF.

I have gone over these many events multiple times, going further into the past and marveling at all the coincidences. The more I learn, the more convinced I become that the footprints of many angels crisscrossed in time, all culminating at the founding of RSF. Angel work collaborated with human work to connect what was already living in spirit with earthly events and matter.

I challenge every founder of any organization that endured to research the events leading up to the actual founding. I am sure any founder will discover these footprints in the biographies involved. I am willing to assert that no successful organization is ever founded without this remarkable choreography guiding events from behind the scene. It is a living design force that moves the people involved more than the people know at the time, and above and beyond their individual volition. The accidental occurrences around all human events reveal angel activity that leaves footprints in specific biographies.

I am convinced that behind every individual biography is a living spiritual collaborator, an angel. Behind every angel is the living choreography of the social fabric, orchestrating our movements, relationships and transactions for the good of the whole. Behind the living choreography as backdrop to human life works the creative design force that moves all of us forward to further development.

37

Sixth Conclusion: Believing Is Seeing

Seeing an angel's footprint is no different than seeing anything else, except that all other causes have to be eliminated. Of course, we have to know where to look. All the biographies, past and present in the world, are the environment in which angels live and work. They leave their footprints all over the world's biographies. There is no sense in looking anywhere else for an angel's footprint than in a human being's biography.

History is the conglomerate of human and angel interworking. Historians traditionally investigate human behavior and natural phenomenon, but angel behavior is carefully eliminated from study. A favorite cause uncovered in history has the name accidental or coincidental ascribed to it. Because it is named we feel the problem of cause to be solved. However, behind the words "accidental" or "coincidental" is the concept "unknown." It would be more honest to say simply, "I don't know!"

The first step in seeing an angel's footprint in a biography is to courageously admit, "I don't know." Seeing an angel's footprints begins by living with the unknown. Of course, acknowledging the unknown has to be based on the question "What causes this event?" The minute one acknowledges an unknown cause or causes, we have admitted to an unknown. All of our knowledge and wisdom rests on questions that we learn to live with and accept. I think it has been proven that nothing can be proven to be true, and that our analytical processes are useful only for proving something to be untrue.

Therefore, everything we know, our entire body of knowledge, simply has not yet been proven untrue. Whatever stands up against our own logic endures as our current knowledge. Knowledge and beliefs have only a very thin membrane between them to distinguish one from the other. In our time, we feel knowledge to be more secure than belief because we have done everything possible to disprove what we know, were unsuccessful and therefore believe it to be true, even as just a working hypothesis.

We all live feeling secure in a world of unknowns. The way we manage to stay sane is to believe. We hang our unknowns on a scaffolding of experience that offers us the illusion of security.

Look at a turning point in any biography. We are approaching an angel's footprint when such questions arise as: "Why did this event come about? What was the nexus of causes?"

A useful sequence of questions follow:

"What really brought this action or reaction about?"

"Why am I not entirely satisfied with all the obvious causes?"

"Why do we still feel something else I can't identify is also involved?"

"Why does this feeling of wonder, surprise, or awe arise every time I recall what actually happened?"

Such questions signify the search for angel activity, and though no answer may come concretely to the fore, just living with the uncertainty develops a feeling that eventually leads to contact with an angel.

As a rule, we can only explain what we do when there is a goal, an intention, a purpose that precedes the action. We are accustomed to explain a subsequent event by identifying a previous element as the cause. Angel footprints are different. The subsequent event causes the earlier consequence into discernible reality. In other words, an angel's footprint appears later in time as the cause of an earlier consequence.

For no apparent reason, you go down 4th Street instead of 3rd Street, which is your usual route. Since there is no reason for you to do that turn, you have no motivating plan or intention that brings it about. In a few steps you encounter a friend who has a problem. That friend with the problem turns out to be the cause of your turning into 4th Street. A SUBSEQUENT EVENT CAUSES A PRIOR ONE. That is often what reveals an angel's footprint.

When you review the events of your life at the end of a day or of a week, or even several years, it is revealing to go backward through the events to discern angel activity combining with human activity. We are co-creators of biography with an angel.

Do we ever see an angel? Rarely! Then only with a special kind of sight not usual for human beings at this stage of development! Can we see their footprints in our life story? Only if we look for them, believe in their existence, and are willing to live knowingly into the unknown.

SECTION SEVEN

BACK IN SCHOOL

"Angel work collaborating with human work connects what is already living in spirit with physical events and material. Every new beginning contains the living spirit connected with a detail of material existence. Matter is never without spirit."

38

Episode 26: The Last Lesson

Ruth and I were both born in Germany, she in Berlin and I near Stuttgart. I was brought to the US at the age of three. She had to experience World War II as a young child and was unable to travel to the U.S. via England until she was eighteen years old. Her route took her through Adelphi College, then Swarthmore College and finally to employment by a literary agency in New York City.

We did not meet until she was 25 years old. We both wrote to our families, "By the time you receive this letter we will be married and living together in an apartment in New York City." None of them took it too badly. It saved everyone a great deal of money and suited our schedule quite well.

A lifetime together with three children, two foster children and a host of visiting children in summertime kept us all busy. Ruth managed everything to do with the household, the children, our social calendar and our wellbeing. I "earned our living" and struggled through a career. None of my efforts would have been possible had it not been for Ruth's tireless energy, her certainty about what was right for all of us, and her lifelong spiritual integrity.

Even later, when she trained in eurythmy and completed her therapeutic eurythmy training in Dornach Switzerland, she still managed the family. For many years, Ruth maintained a therapeutic eurythmy practice, working closely with doctors and helping as many as seventeen patients a day in her studio, at Waldorf schools in the area and at workshops given by doctors.

Her lifetime was one of service. She loved biographies, loved people's stories and devoted herself to helping them. Her youngest patient was just 5 years old, while her oldest turned out to be 90. All ages revered her. All illnesses and failings were eased and even overcome by her deep ministrations. If anyone could, she understood health and illness while devoting herself to healing body and soul. Since the spirit is always healthy, her healing worked.

Cancer took all of us by surprise! Even I found it hard to believe. At first there was a little bleeding and then pain. She agreed to receive chemotherapy and then radiation, to no avail. An operation was necessary, which left her with an ostomy. Starting in January 2007, we began our struggle to figure out how to deal with wafers and pouches. Several times, we had disastrous accidents. Fortunately there was almost always someone else around to help with the worst of it. We consulted friends with similar illnesses to find out about their experiences and how they coped. Surgeons only operate. They are excellent at finite procedures, but not with how you cope with everything that has changed. We were at the beginning of a new kind of unknown.

Two months after the operation, Ruth had a mild stroke. Doctors were unable to determine the cause and concluded it was simply due to a brief spell of very high blood pressure. After a week in the hospital, she returned to our apartment with frequent dizzy spells and hesitation in walking, especially climbing even just one step.

A month after the operation, Ruth continued suffering from reflux. It burned her throat and tasted vile. Every meal began to be a fearful exercise, in anticipation as well as in actuality, and certainly afterward. How could she go on like this? Something must be wrong.

The tests at first offered some hope, but shortly thereafter, a second test was needed. The doctors concluded that it was cancer of the esophagus, a totally different kind of cancer from the first. Chemotherapy and radiation were not an option this time. Only an operation offered some hope.

In June of 2007, only five months after the first operation, Ruth had her esophagus removed, leaving only a short stump. The stomach was pulled up and connected to it. Very few doctors knew how to do this, and many questioned its use. We spoke with several people who had undergone the operation and became hopeful.

The operation was a success, but the reflux continued. It was another year before it became manageable and thereafter occurred only mildly and infrequently. However, her confidence in life had been shaken. So many operations, so much anesthesia, so much disappointment and worry left Ruth uncertain about her connection with the Earth. She had difficulty walking. Her knees often pained her and did not hold her upright. We began a long saga of doctor visits and specialists advising us. We slowly learned to keep our own counsel and take whatever herbal and natural remedies we could safely believe in.

During 2007 and 2008 and beyond, my life also changed dramatically. I was not able to serve many of my clients. My first book *Money Can Heal* had just been published. I could not do any book signings, nor could I engage in lectures and workshops associated with the book. I began to wonder what had taken my life away so completely. Where had it gone? My days were full. I did the shopping, and since our diet changed frequently it required many trips a week. I did the cooking of all three meals, breakfast, lunch and dinner, although we ate our main meal in the middle of the day and only a light supper in the evening.

Ruth went from a cane to a walker and sometimes a wheelchair. I was needed whenever she had to move in the apartment or outside. What normally took ten or fifteen minutes now needed 30 to 40 minutes if not an hour.

Ruth was miserable that she took so much of my time. Whatever she could do herself became a matter of urgency and pride. Nevertheless, getting in and out of bed, moving from the sofa to the dining room table and daily walks all took time and attention. All along, I kept feeling that my life was being taken away from me. I couldn't do any of the things I wanted to do, but was occupied all day with things I *had* to do.

One day while I was feeling especially sorry for myself, I fell into a deep hole and wondered if I would ever find my way out and back into a life. How could I justify my existence to myself, my clients, my readers and my family if I am never able to get anything done? Ruth felt even more miserable. She blamed herself for needing me so much and taking me away from my "work."

In the middle of depression, an idea descended on me and hung around me with a warm and friendly light. "Suppose this actually is my life?" It floated there above me and quietly insisted on my attention. "Suppose, indeed, this is really my life!"

I was only 77 years old, but wasn't it possible, without my realizing it, that I had again entered a new and challenging section of my life? Maybe there was something important to experience, as there had been in all the other sections. I had plunged into every other segment with a full heart, eagerly awaiting the next lesson. This one I had been dragged into backward, kicking and screaming under the pressure of "duty."

I found a way to turn myself around and welcome what was now my life. Caring for a single human being was definitely acting locally, but I needed to think globally. Suppose all that I had done previously—operating in the public and strutting about in an aura of my own importance was actually much less meaningful than taking on the care of one single person and doing it with love?

Suppose I could take this part of my life and penetrate it deeply with love and compassion, would it change the world? RSF Social Finance has as its mission "to change how the world works with money." Who can judge what brings about the greatest impact on the world and humanity?

Every time I used to work in my garden, I would begin by looking around and assessing the situation. I would start noticing everything that needed to be done: the weeds to pull, earth to aerate, shrubs to trim, fruit trees and berries to prune. The list goes on and on. I am already exhausted, even though I haven't done a stitch of work. Nothing happens until I bend over and pull a single weed. Everything follows from that single act performed in a single square inch of my garden, and yet in the end it all gets done. Every new beginning has to focus on a detail to forge the pathway leading to enormous change.

Perhaps caring for a single human being is the act for which the whole world waits. Could it be that everything else we do has an element of self-serving in it, and it is only when we truly serve that this vast spatial vacuum of the world is warmed and enhanced? Is this new task of mine what truly transforms the world?

In the world balance, my shift from macro to micro signals the entire universe that a new beginning has taken place. The world vibrates in synch with such an act. It spreads its warmth from heart to heart and changes all for the better.

Can I take this new life and bring complete acceptance to it? How deep can my commitment become? How much genuine feeling can I bring to bear on every single detail of my new task?

If I am right, then there is hope in every single act of labor, regardless of its scope and expense. The dishwasher in a restaurant should be able to change the world. The cook could instill a level of love into his/her task to uplift the whole of humanity. Every form of labor may actually contain within it the forces of transformation. Perhaps what I am doing with my new life is the most significant of all my activities. Perhaps my biography has culminated in the highest point of achievement, if I can only pull it off successfully. I plunged headlong into my greatest challenge.

Now, I finally understood my relationship to my Angel. She was the model for what a human being can become. She, in being linked so closely to me, demonstrated care giving in its true essence. At the end of our evolution, when all of us had passed through a long development, we might have taken over the angel's current work, freed her to move on into the next stage, leaving us to care for each other, care for the earth and all that lived within it and transformed ourselves into ultimate caregivers. Would we then be invisible? Who then would be human? With whom then would we be linked, engaged in their development and forced to suffer the consequences of their learning?

The great ladder into the divine that Jacob climbed suddenly made sense. It's the way the universe is formed. It's not a circle at all; it's an ever-lengthening ladder to be climbed individually and together. What matters in a life is no longer the list of ordinary and extraordinary achievements. They are simply the means by which we accomplish our true goal; to transform ourselves into what already lives in us as love.